Assessing and Treating

Trauma and PTSD

Linda J. Schupp, Ph.D.

PESI, LCC strives to obtain knowledgeable authors and faculty for its
publications and seminars. The clinical recommendations contained
herein are the result of extensive author research and review. Obviously,
any recommendations for patient care must be held up against individual
circumstances at hand. To the best of our knowledge any recommendations included by the author or faculty reflect currently accepted practice.
However, these recommendations cannot be considered universal and
complete. The authors and publisher repudiate any responsibility for
unfavorable effects that result from information, recommendations,
undetected omissions or errors. Professionals using this publication
should research other original sources of authority as well.

**For information on this and other PESI publications,
please call 800-843-7763 or
visit our website at www.pesi.com**

ACKNOWLEDGEMENTS

This book is lovingly dedicated to the memory of two significant people who profoundly influenced my life, Charles S. Adams and Linda Siler Adams, who adopted me as their very own child during the first few months of my life. They gave me all the love and nurturance an infant could ever want or need. It has been said that self esteem is built when a child *"feels"* loved, not necessarily when a child is loved. The difference in being loved or feeling loved lies in the parent's ability to express the love in the way the child can internalize it. My precious parents were specialists in doing all the things I needed to feel loved, valued, and approved. In doing so, they gave me the priceless gift of self worth. Had I not felt significant or whole, I may not have been able to survive the tragedies that lay ahead of me. The stability, security and essential sense of self that they lovingly constructed in me became my sails in the storms of life. If they can peek through heaven's portals, I hope they know how thankful I am that God allowed me to have such wonderful parents.

I am also indebted to Pat Patterson for her skill of translating illegible notes into a readable text, and for typing and retyping the many versions of this manuscript. I also want to thank my editor, Andrew Clausen, my publisher PESI Healthcare, and Michael Olson, Project Manager of Mental Health Education, who expressed the need for this book and trusted me to write it.

I would be remiss if I didn't acknowledge my many clients and friends who allowed me to walk the trauma pathway with them. Their trust in me as a co-sufferer enabled them to express the unexpressable, and brought some measure of healing, meaning, and wholeness to their lives and mine. In addition, I am ever grateful to the myriad of dedicated health care professionals who have so tirelessly given of themselves to the often unacknowledged task of *"healing the hurting."* I applaud you for your competence, perseverance, and commitment!

Linda J. Schupp, Ph.D., B.C.E.T.S. is a nationally and internationally known speaker, who has trained tens of thousands of people in her seminars. She holds a Ph.D. in Psychology, an M.A. in Clinical Psychology, an M.Ed. in Guidance and Counseling, and is a Board Certified Expert in Traumatic Stress. Dr. Schupp has been counseling, lecturing, and speaking for over 35 years, and is gifted at incorporating her psychological background with an entertaining flair for the humorous and dramatic.

She is currently working at Regis University with Master's level psychology students and in 1996, Regis University honored her with the prestigious "Excellence in Teaching Award." Dr. Schupp is also serving as adjunct faculty for The Union Institute and University Graduate College School of Professional Psychology where she works with Ph.D. Psychology students.

Dr. Schupp maintains a private practice specializing in trauma, and employs Eye Movement Desensitization Reprocessing to treat traumatic stress, depression, anxiety, and Post-Traumatic Stress Disorder. She has shared her trauma and grief seminars with many of the survivors and workforce personnel involved in the Oklahoma City bombing, and she continues to provide counseling service to individuals affected by the Columbine High School shootings.

Dr. Schupp has authored two previous books titled *Grief: Normal, Complicated, and Traumatic,* and *False Comforters: Words That Wound, and Helps That Heal.* She has also produced a CD and training video titled, *Is There Life After Loss?* which is applicable for professional and lay counselors. In addition, PESI has recorded her and produced an audio titled *Working with Survivors of Traumatic Stress.* She possesses audios and videos on a variety of other topics and has made numerous radio and television appearances. This current book focuses on the many faces of trauma which present themselves in a multitude of disorders; some easily recognized and diagnosed, others hidden behind criteria that doesn't address their etiology of trauma.

Personally speaking, Linda has suffered the traumatic loss of her mother, father, two husbands and a son. These and other trauma-related experiences have given her a heart full of compassion and a mind filled with wisdom, which brings depth, knowledge, and understanding to the field of traumatology.

TABLE OF CONTENTS

Preface

The experience of trauma produces exhaustion on many levels. Trauma survivors are physiologically, emotionally, cognitively, and sometimes spiritually depleted. Their sympathetic nervous systems are vigilantly scanning the environment for varied stimuli, ready to fight, flee, or freeze at the slightest provocation. The trauma-related emotions of fear, anxiety, and depression take their toll on energy reserves. Cognitive processes may seem like the survivor is *"functioning in a fog."* Concentration, focus, and decision making can be exasperating and exhausting. If the trauma has challenged deeply-held beliefs about God or philosophies about how the world should operate, then the bombardment and shattering of these security bases have left survivors in the field of desolation.

Is my description of the experience of trauma purely theoretical, perhaps written from the comfortable environment of my office chair, or have I experienced any of those symptoms while residing in the *"laboratory of life?"* The theoretical understanding has been a personal journey for me and I have been imprisoned by traumatic episodes for portions of my life.

At one point in time, I had buried five out of my six immediate family members, having only my precious daughter Jackie remaining in this life. Heaven was much richer for the addition of my loved ones, but earth was poverty-stricken for me. As many wise theorists have noted in the past, it isn't just the deaths of loved ones that create great pain, it is also the horrific circumstances surrounding the deaths.

Trauma, by nature, overwhelms our capacity to endure and leaves us feeling helpless and powerless. I fully identified with such responses, and often wondered what I could do to stop the tirade of untimely deaths. I was a stranger as to loved ones dying peaceful deaths from old age; all my family members were snatched from me in shocking, unexpected ways. My mother was hit by an out-of-control car circling down a spiral ramp of a parking deck and the impact hurled her through a storefront window. She lingered unconscious for five days, then died. Later in life, my father died from a medical mistake in a nursing home. He pitifully begged the attending personnel to stop the procedure, but his cries went unheard. His heart stopped instead.

I have also experienced the untimely deaths of two husbands. The husband of my youth went to sleep at the wheel of his car, which crashed into an embankment on the side of the road and folded like an accordion. Despite the impact, there wasn't a broken bone in his body; however, the internal injuries were severe and he died before I could arrive at the hospital. Later in life, I faced the traumatic death of another husband through suicide. Upon returning home from work I found him alive, but unconscious, in our garage which was filled with fumes of carbon monoxide. Attempts to save his life were all in vain.

As traumatic as those losses were, my most severe psychological wounding occurred with a terminal diagnosis of a synovial sarcoma in the right arm of my son, Cliff. The first line of treatment was the amputation of the entire arm followed by many rounds of radiation and chemotherapy. Although he outlived the physician's projections, after six long years a blood clot to the heart took his life.

Friends and loved ones did what they could to comfort my daughter and I, but well intentioned words and advice falls flat in the face of such trauma. At times I listened to others, and found myself wandering in the wrong direction while searching for the path to healing. Some misguided turns in the road only led to deeper despair.

The old adage, *"Physician, heal thyself"* certainly was applicable to me, and I am thankful that I can present my *"reconstructed self"* to a hurting world as a hopeful and humble survivor. Many elements contributed to my reconstruction on a physiological, cognitive, emotional, and spiritual level. During my times of intense grief, I made a conscious decision to *"search for meaning, not happiness."* Interestingly enough, happiness often follows as a byproduct. How do we receive any meaning from such senseless and devastating pain? We diligently search for it. To redeem the grief and trauma requires one to make creative use of it. I have purposed in my present life that my tears will serve as waves of movement that thrust me forward towards others of like suffering.

Trauma creates a *"vacuum in the soul"* which can remain empty or be filled with compassion and care. I am not unique in this dedication or perseverance. Many wounded healers have gone before me and I am simply following in their footsteps. Many trauma specialists are *"there"* because *"they have been there."* If I can ease someone's burden, shed light on the way, walk the stony pathway with them, listen to the pain and devastation of the trauma, carry them through the dangerous and treacherous hills and valleys, or simply love them through the process, then my journey has been a meaningful venture.

Introduction

The fingers of trauma have invaded every segment of society and because of its pervasiveness, trauma has become a multidisciplinary concern and emphasis. Traumatologists predict that 70–90% of people will either witness, be exposed to or experience a trauma sometime during their life. Trauma parades in many costumes, wearing diverse faces and occupying numerous forms, some more obvious than others. Natural disasters, combat, murders, terrorism, bombings, shootings, and car accidents are frequent occurrences, often on public display in newspapers, television, and the media. Other trauma occurs behind closed doors and its insidious effects evidence in numerous disturbances such as borderline, antisocial, and narcissistic personality disorders, obsessive compulsive disorder, or dissociative identity disorder. Who can calculate the impact of physical and sexual child abuse that is secretive, repeated, and prolonged? The physical body of the child may survive and develop into adulthood, but the crime of *"soul murder"* may remain undetected, unpunished, and untreated.

And what about the hidden traumatic relationships that surface in our clinics or offices as depression or panic disorders, and belie the truth of their real identity of trauma? Many medical and mental health clinics, religious institutions, governmental agencies, and charitable organizations, to name a few, have heard the disguised cries of women, and sometimes men, suffering from physical, mental, emotional, verbal, financial, or sexual abuse. These victims are often so deeply traumatized that they lose their independent sense of self and bond with the perpetrator, thus continuing the cycle of abuse.

What resources are available to attend to the myriad of needs that trauma victims present? What treatments are able to transform victims into survivors? Who will be there to pick up the pieces of shattered lives and reconstruct them into meaningful living? Those of us who are dedicated to the field of traumatology will arrive and respond from a multitude of occupations to fill that overwhelming need.

Treatments also present themselves from diverse theoretical orientations, providing clinicians with a vast eclectic approach. It is imperative that health care professionals avail themselves of the most current physiological and psychological approaches. To competently serve our clients, we must keep abreast of the contributions from many fields. For instance, it was previously believed that once neurons had been destroyed in the brain, they couldn't be regrown. Current neurological research has dispelled that myth and provided new understanding regarding the possibility of regrowth. Many trauma specialists are now viewing Post Traumatic Stress Disorder and other trauma-related syndromes as neurological disorders caused by traumatic stress.

Based on this neurological research, psychopharmacology has taken its proper place in the array of treatments and has much to offer. Accelerated information processing also presents numerous techniques that hasten the healing and minimize the pain of trauma. Healthcare professionals can currently choose from a vast array of beneficial treatments.

Trauma has always existed and will continue to exist, so it behooves those of us in the helping professions to prepare ourselves. This book serves as a practical guide for the *"tried and true"* therapies, and for the newer innovative approaches to trauma. I applaud each of you for your dedication to your particular field of service, and for your interest in the integration of traumatology with your present work. Hopefully, with this multidisciplinary approach we can make a difference in the lives of traumatized clients.

CHAPTER ONE

The Nature of Traumatic Stress

THE ETIOLOGY OF STRESS AND TRAUMATIC STRESS

Prior to the 1960s, the word *"stress"* was relatively unknown. Today it is a commonly used term in every avenue of life. The early research focused primarily on the affects of stress on the body. Even today, many experts consider it as a cause of disease and illness in 80% of cases. Stress can be the culprit in major situations such as cancer and heart disease and in such irritating conditions as warts. Dr. Hans Selye, a European physician and physiologist, coined the first definition in the 1920s to explain what he observed in his patients.

> Stress is the nonspecific response of the body to any demand placed upon it to adapt.

> Hans Selye 1956/1976

He later refined it to include pleasurable events as well.

> Stress is the nonspecific response of the body to any demand placed upon it to adapt, whether that demand produced pleasure or pain.

> Hans Selye 1976

Current theories have included other stress affected areas in addition to the body. Stress can also impact people mentally, emotionally, and spiritually.

Brian Luke Seaward (1999) reminds clinicians that Selye's definition combined with Richard Lazarus (1984) has been expanded by the holistic medicine field.

> Stress is the inability to cope with a perceived (real or imagined) threat to one's physical, mental, emotional, and spiritual well being.
>
> Brian Luke Seaward 1999

Life itself cannot be lived without people experiencing stress as either a cause or as an effect. Reber (1995) in The Penguin Dictionary of Psychology provides us with his definition.

> 1. Generally, any force that when applied to a system causes some significant modification of its form, usually with the connotation that the modification is a deformation or a distortion. The term is used with respect to physical, psychological, and social forces and pressures. Note that stress in this sense refers to a cause; stress is the antecedent of some effect.
>
> 2. A state of psychological tension produced by the kinds of forces or pressures alluded to in 1 above. Note that stress in this sense is an effect; stress is the result of other pressures. When meaning two is intended, the term stressor is typically used for the causal agent.

Stress is sometimes viewed as either a constructive or destructive force. The difference in the two lies in the outcome. Constructive stress leads people to a better place in some facet of life without detrimental effects on the person, while destructive stress leaves them incapacitated after the stressful time period. For instance, Dan, a manager of a large computer firm, decided to attend an evening college class to acquire a new job skill. He temporarily felt the extra pressure during the semester of the course, but after its completion reaped the rewards of a new career promotion. In analyzing his situation, we can observe that the stress was not unduly prolonged and produced a desired result. The entrance to college may have been perceived initially as a physical and mental threat, but Dan succeeded and was no worse for the experience. Viewing constructive stress in a humorous vein, we might conclude *"There's light at the end of the tunnel and it's not a train."* Most people need just enough tension to function at the highest level, but not so much that they break in the process.

Dr. Walter Cannon (1914), a contemporary of Hans Selye, indicated that during stress the person experiences the *"fight or flight"* syndrome. Selye (1956) coined the phrase General Adaptation Syndrome to explain the process which occurs. This syndrome sets the accompanying physiological, mental, and emotional arousal systems in motion. A modern, more inclusive version of Dr. Cannon's term might rename it the *"fight, flight, or freeze syndrome"* which identifies a new component. Freezing or taking an inactive, passive stance could occur in many instances in stress and traumatic stress. There are many everyday examples of a mild freezing response. For instance, Johnny doesn't move or fight back as his bigger brother bends his arm behind his back. A passive stance may prevent the further damage of a broken arm. We often observe this passivity in the animal kingdom as a small dog stops fighting and bares his throat to the conquering dog. Freezing becomes increasingly important when used as a survival mechanism in traumatic circumstances such as the child who submits to repeated sexual abuse, because the threat of a beating for non-compliance is more frightening than the abuse.

How do everyday stress responses compare with traumatic stress responses? There are clear boundary lines between the two areas. Traumatic stress is a heightened form of stress which is preceded by a trauma, an event that is considered life-threatening to self or others. Traumatic stress also occurs with multiple or repeated trauma. It is characterized in the DSM-IV-TR by an emotional response of *"fear, helplessness, or horror."* Reber (1995) in The Penguin Dictionary of Psychology explains that the word trauma has its origin in the Greek word *"wound."* It is

> a term used freely either for physical injury caused by some direct external force or for psychological injury caused by some extreme emotional assault.

For purposes of this book, trauma will be viewed primarily as a severe psychological wounding that is considered shocking and memorable and according to the DSM-IV-TR, it would *"evoke significant symptoms of distress in most people."* Mark Lerner (2001) with the American Academy of Experts in Traumatic Stress provides a current definition

Traumatic stress refers to the emotional, cognitive, behavioral, and physiological experience of individuals who are exposed to, or who witness, events that overwhelm their coping and problem-solving abilities.

Rachael Yehuda and Alexander McFarlane (1995) draw some distinctions between Selye's stress response and the Post-traumatic Stress Disorder (PTSD) experience.

It is now clear that PTSD does provide a model for a process of adjustment and destabilization to trauma that has biological, psychological, and phenomenological dimensions. The biological investigations have demonstrated that the substrates of the disorder may not, in fact, be similar to the 'normative stress response' described by Selye, but rather, may be a progressive sensitization of biological systems that leave the individual hyperresponsive to a variety of stimuli.

THE AROUSAL ZONES

Traumatic stress, the accelerated form of stress, encompasses the total person and affects all areas of functioning. The Modulation Model (Ogden, P. & Kekuni, M., 2000) demonstrates a person's ability to tolerate stress. In non-traumatic stress, whether positive or negative, the person usually resides within the optimum arousal zone (Wilbarger & Wilbarger, 1997). Bessel van der Kolk (1987) states that traumatized individuals display poor tolerance in relationship to arousal. They are unable to remain within a normal range. Dr. van der Kolk (1987) explains that the traumatized person may exist above or below the optimum arousal zone, or swing uncontrollably between the two zones. A bi-phasic alternation would move between hyperarousal and hypoarousal (numbing/freezing). When individuals live in either of those zones, then upper levels of processing are ineffective. Dissociation may occur. **(Please see charts on page 5.)** These zones contribute to two sets of defensive behaviors. Ogden (2000) clarifies the distinctions between hyperactive and passive responses.

THE MODULATION MODEL
OPTIMUM AROUSAL ZONE
Figure 1

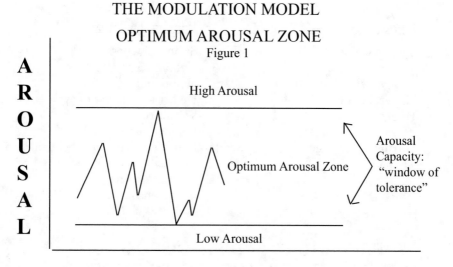

THE MODULATION MODEL
THE BI-PHASIC RESPONSE TO TRAUMA
Figure 2

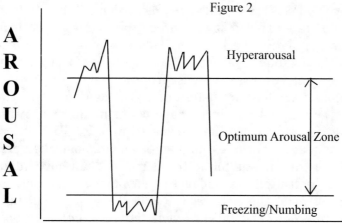

Reprinted by permission of: Ogden, P. & Kekuni, M. (2000). "Sensorimotor Psychotherapy: One Method for Processing Traumatic Memory." *Traumatology* Vol. VI, Issue 3, Article 3. Boulder, CO: Sensorimotor Psychotherapy Institute and Naropa University.

EFFECTS OF BI-PHASIC RESPONSE

Hyperactive Defenses	**Passive Defenses**
Defensiveness	Submissiveness
Aggressiveness	Helplessness
(against self or others)	No boundaries
Hyperalertness	Feelings of inadequacy
Hypervigilance	Victim role stance
Excessive motor activity	Unquestioned obedience
Uncontrolled rage	Repeated victim role behaviors
	Lifeless, non-expressive
	mannerisms
	No defense system

PREDICTORS AND PREDISPOSITIONS TO POST-TRAUMATIC STRESS DISORDER AND TRAUMATIC STRESS

It is difficult to ascertain who are the most vulnerable or likely candidates to develop Post-Traumatic Stress Disorder (PTSD). In fact, A.S. Blank (1993) stated that it is dangerous to provide generalizations about this population because there are too many variables among people, the traumatic events themselves, and the circumstances surrounding the events. There is an additional problem when we limit a diagnosis to the parameters of PTSD as defined in the DSM-IV-TR. Many trauma survivors have components of a stress syndrome but do not experience the full spectrum of PTSD. Rachael Yehuda and Alexander McFarlane (1995) cite epidemiological studies in the aftermath of trauma and found that survivors can have intrusive memories of the trauma, as well as some avoidance phenomena, yet they would not meet the criteria of PTSD. They pose the theoretical question, *are there specific symptoms that differentiate people who survive a traumatic experience without being disabled from those who become severely symptomatic?* Much research in the present is still attempting to answer this question.

Differences of opinion existed even among the early researchers. Edouard Stierlin (1901, 1911), a Swiss psychiatrist, was the first researcher to study a non-clinical populations' reaction to disaster. After the 1907 earthquake in Messina, Italy which killed 70,000 of its inhabitants, he observed that no previous psychopathological predisposition was required to render a *traumatic neurosis* diagnosis. The event itself was quite sufficient to produce great psychological distress.

Bonhoeffer (1926), a German psychiatrist, totally disagreed with Stierlin and felt that traumatic neurosis wasn't an illness but a means to acquire compensation from the government. However, he did think certain individuals were predisposed to what he termed *"compensation neurosis."*

Ariel Y. Shalev (1996) summarized 38 studies which focused on five primary influences that predicted whether or not a victim developed PTSD.

1. Pretrauma vulnerability
2. Magnitude of the stressor
3. Preparedness for the event
4. Quality of the immediate and short term responses
5. Post event 'recovery' factors

ARIEL Y. SHALEV, 1996
<u>STUDY SUMMARIES</u>

*PREDICTORS OF PTSD AND OTHER TRAUMA RELATED SYNDROMES**

- Severity of injury
- Torture
- Rapes by strangers; use of physical force or weapons; injury
- (PTSD): participation in atrocities; cumulative exposure to combat stressors
- Family history of antisocial behavior; female gender
- (Exposure): lower education; male gender; early conduct problems; extraversion; family history of psychiatric disorder

---

* Data from Shalev, Arieh Y. (1996). *"Stress versus Traumatic Stress: From Acute Homeostatic Reactions to Chronic Psychopathology"* in van der Kolk, Bessel, McFarlane, Alexander C., and Weisaeth, Lars (eds.) *Traumatic Stress: The Effects of Overwhelming Experience on Mind, Body, and Society,* (pp. 83-85), New York: Guilford Press.

- (PTSD): early separation from parents; neuroticism; pre-existing anxiety or depression; family history of anxiety
- Combat intensity and duration; physical injury
- Poor preservice relationships; being wounded; friends missing in action (MIA); guilt over death of a friend; lack of preparation to leave the unit; failure to discuss feelings on return
- (PTSD): war trauma; resettlement strain
- (Depression): recent stressful events
- Job instability, family history of psychiatric illness; parental poverty; history of child abuse; parental separation prior to age 10
- Distress postinjury
- Combat exposure; military adjustment; MMPI scores; anxiety
- Traumatic violence; distress at having participated in such acts
- History of mental health problems; aggressiveness of assault; belief that people are not trustworthy; conservatism regarding sex
- Combat exposure (nine-fold increase in prevalence from non-combat to high combat exposure)
- Intensity of the stressor; exposure to grotesque death; level of education; social support at homecoming
- Combat intensity; current impact of previously experienced events, concurrent level of life stress
- (PTSD): Life threat during crime; physical injury; completed rape
- Combat exposure; exposure to abusive violence and killing; subjective "experiential" coping
- Negative parenting behaviors predict PTSD symptom severity at lower levels of combat exposure
- Combat exposure; age at war zone duty; duration of war zone duty; physical injury
- Introversion, neuroticism; family history of psychiatric disorder
- Level of exposure; guilt; knowing the child who was killed
- Childhood histories of abuse and family fighting

- Predisaster psychiatric disorder; Major Depressive Disorders (MDD) predicted PTSD in women but not men
- Total body surface area burn; female sex; lack of responsibility for the injury
- Subjective variables: emotional distress, perceived social support
- High crime stress; significant interaction among crime stress level; precrime depression and PTSD
- (PTSD symptoms): Minnesota Multiphasic Personality Inventory (MMPI) scales of hypochondriasis, psychopathy, masculinity-femininity, and paranoia
- (PTSD) depression, hypomania, and social introversion
- Predisaster psychiatric histories predict post disaster psychiatric disorders
- Combat experience; perceptions of homecoming
- Social support; life events; internal locus of control
- Blunting coping strategies
- Proportion body weight lost during captivity; experience of torture
- Confinement; weight loss; lower socioeconomic status; greater hardship; lower military rank
- History of physical abuse

As with every physical or mental condition, the outcome will vary from one client to another. There are many variables that are interwoven within the fabric of the person that affect the prognosis.

Dr. Mark D. Lerner of The American Academy of Experts in Traumatic Stress (2002) provides us with the following list of potential indicators for PTSD.

*"HIGH RISK" INDICATORS FOR POST-TRAUMATIC STRESS DISORDER (PTSD)**

- prior exposure to severe adverse life events (e.g., combat)
- prior victimization (e.g., childhood sexual and physical abuse)
- significant losses

---

* Reprinted with permission of The American Academy of Experts in Traumatic Stress (www.aaets.org).

- close proximity to the event
- extended exposure to danger
- pre-trauma anxiety and depression
- chronic medical condition
- substance involvement
- history of trouble with authority (e.g., stealing, vandalism, etc.)
- mental illness
- lack of familial/social support
- having no opportunity to vent (i.e., unable to tell one's story)
- strong emotional reactions upon exposure to the event
- physically injured by event, etc.

Most theorists, researchers, and trauma specialists unanimously believe that *"dose-response"* is an accurate predictor of who will develop some form of traumatic stress. The experience could be sexual abuse, rape, natural disaster, terrorism, domestic violence, combat, accidents, or other traumas, but the common denominator is the dose response. The greater the exposure to horrific sights, sounds, and smells as well as the threat to one's life, the more likely it is the person will develop PTSD or some other trauma-related condition. It is safe to conclude that individuals who are directly exposed to dangerous life-threatening events have the highest risk of suffering traumatic stress effects.

Most theorists and clinicians believe that pre-existing psychiatric/psychological conditions or biological factors could increase vulnerability. Friedman (2001) indicates that gender is also a factor. He explains that women are twice as likely to develop PTSD as men probably because women have experienced more interpersonal abuse where there has been a perpetrator. This type of abuse, particularly repeated abuse, is a more accurate predictor of PTSD than the impersonal or impartial traumatic effects of natural disasters. Age at which a trauma occurs is another variable; for instance, child abuse in any form such as physical, sexual, verbal, economic, or separation from a parent sets one up for PTSD or for what Judith Herman (1992) termed Complex PTSD. Young adults under age 25 are also at risk. Even genetics seem to predispose one to PTSD or to protect from it. Of course, a diagnosis of Acute Stress Disorder (ASD) could serve as a predictor since 83% of ASD sufferers do develop PTSD (Brewin, et al., 1999). Veterans of war who witnessed or participated in atrocities have increased risk, as do civilians and children who were involved in war experiences. There are some studies which show that those without a college education are also at risk. Of course, previous trauma experiences prior to the current one would predispose the individual to PTSD, as well as damaging life circumstances such as deaths of loved ones, job loss, financial problems, or divorce.

Kessler, et al. (1995) has shown that 8% of people living in the United States have suffered with PTSD due to such traumas as childhood abuse, natural disasters, car accidents, rapes, assault, and a variety of additional traumas. Bremner (2002) states that *"16% of women are sexually abused before their 18th birthdays, and about half as many men, which means that about 50 million individuals in this country were severely abused in childhood."* Bremner, Vermetten, and Mazure (2000) have revealed in their research that emotional abuse and neglect may be as damaging as sexual abuse.

Mark Friedman (2001) states that approximately 40% of PTSD sufferers will not recover even if they received treatment. This doesn't mean they haven't shown improvement, but the disorder will remain throughout their lifetime in a severe chronic state. Some clinicians disagree with this percentage, and with new treatments and medications, perhaps many more will be helped. Regardless of the percentages, there will be those clients that will have some degree of impairment throughout their life.

THE BRAIN, BODY, AND MIND CONNECTION

Bessel van der Kolk (1994) explains that the *"brain, body, and mind are inextricably linked, and it is only for heuristic reasons that we can still speak of them as if they constitute separate entities. Alterations in any one of these three will ultimately affect the other two."*

Dr. Douglas Bremner (2002) provides us with a summary regarding the inter-relatedness of the mind, brain, and body in respect to traumatic experiences.

> [U]p until now, there has been a false dichotomy between physical and mental disease. It is artificial to separate mind and brain, physical and mental, and that the effects of psychological trauma on the individual needs to be considered in neurological terms. The same processes stimulated by

stress responses that may lead to depression and behavioral changes are mediated by stress responsive systems like cortisol and catecholamines that also have effects on physical health such as heart disease and infection.

Dr. Douglas Bremner 2002

Bremner (2002) states that what an individual *"sees, hears, smells, and feels"* then travels through perceptions and is modified by prior memories, emotions, and beliefs. It then is processed by the nervous system and becomes a neurological response and a new set of memories and cognitions. He continues to explain that these events have *"effects on cardiovascular, immunological, and metabolic function."*

What does this information mean to the myriad of occupations of health care professionals that treat trauma? The answer is simple; these professionals must envision the entire scope of the impact of trauma. Tunnel vision doesn't work; a more comprehensive approach must be employed if the client is properly treated. A holistic model of health should be adopted where we provide a network of referrals to our clients so that the whole person is addressed. For instance, a mental health counselor working with a survivor of traumatic stress would ensure that the client has an existing network of medical professionals who are aware of and working on the physiological aspects of the trauma. The reverse is also true where medical professionals can refer a client to mental health professionals. If diverse occupations remain isolated and focus only on their specialty, then the client is not truly served and total healing may not occur. Isolation in our occupations is an injustice to our clients.

NEUROBIOLOGICAL CHANGES IN THE BRAIN

Current research has proven that traumatic stress can have detrimental effects on brain structure and function. J. Douglas Bremner (2002) has conducted extensive research on the neurological effects of extreme stress. He reminds us that

The brain areas most sensitive to stress are the same systems that we call upon for survival in a situation of extreme threat, such as the norepinephrine and cortisol systems. These brain areas are very sensitive to the effects of stress. Traumatic stressors have neurological consequences that in turn mediate symptoms of stress-related psychiatric disorders like PTSD and depression. Brain areas involved in memory also play a critical role in the stress response.

Walter Cannon's (1927) fight or flight syndrome provides a picture of the kinds of stress-related responses a person might employ. If a threat is conveyed from the amygdala to the hypothalamus, then the hypothalamus sets the fight or flight response in motion. Whenever we encounter a life threatening event, be it human, animal, or inanimate object, our body releases enormous amounts of epinephrine, norepinephrine, and cortisol to provide the energy to fight or flee. The locus coeruleus in the brain stem also floods the brain with norepinephrine to provide increased alertness and ability to act. Numerous neurological researchers agree that we need those chemicals for survival, but too much of them negatively affects the brain, causing it to malfunction. With long term traumatic stress, these systems keep pumping out too much of these stimulants and don't shut down when the threat is abated.

Cortisol, one of the survival chemicals rearranges the distribution of our energy to assist with prolonged stress. Bremner (2002) states that it increases our heart rate, raises our blood pressure, provides oxygen and strength to the muscles and brain, supplies more serum glucose, causes free fatty acid coagulation, and enhances blood coagulation ability, to name a few of the essential physiological changes.

Bremner (2002) explains that elevated levels of the stress hormone cortisol can damage the hippocampus, a seahorse-shaped organ in the limbic cortex in the temporal lobe, which is involved in learning and memory. Elevated cortisol also affects mood which leads to depression and feelings of fatigue. Bruce McEwen, et al. (1992), Robert Sapolsky, (1996), Uno, Tarara, Else, Suleman, and Sapolsky (1989) have also conducted studies that clearly substantiate the negative effects of stress-released cortisol (glucocorticoids) on the brain.

In addition, Robert Sapolsky's experiments on monkeys also revealed that severe stress damaged the hippocampus, causing problems with memory. Bremner (2002) reiterates that *"stress may have resulted in damage to the hippocampus in PTSD patients, and that this could explain the memory problems . . ."* He noted that his PTSD patients had problems with new learning and current memory tasks, yet past memories prior to PTSD were intact. These individuals demonstrated similarities to patients suffering from what Bremner termed *neurological amnesia*.

Bremner, Randall, Scott, et al.(1995) found that in studies with veterans diagnosed with PTSD, the hippocampus was smaller than normal. The more memory problems, the smaller the hippocampus. These findings were substantiated by magnetic resonance imaging (MRI), which clearly revealed the reduction in size of the hippocampus. Bremner, Randall, Capelli, et al. (1995) also measured the size of the hippocampus in adults who were severely physically or sexually abused as children, and found the same memory problems, and a reduced hippocampus.

Stein, et al. (1997) also discovered hippocampal reductions in sexually abused women diagnosed with PTSD. Stein's work revealed that dissociative symptoms were due to hippocampus atrophy. Bremner (2002) states that in traumatized patients, the greatest decreases in volume of the hippocampus are associated with the most pronounced symptoms of dissociation. It appears that prolonged traumatic stress is the essential ingredient in structural changes of the hippocampus. This is not to say that other components are not important. Traumatic stress is frequently accompanied by depression, which also causes hippocampus decreases. Sheline, et al. (1996) and Bremner, Narayan, et al. (2000) attest to that finding in their research. The hippocampus also holds the memory of the emotions related to the context of the event. It is designed to protect us from further threats of a similar nature by stimulating the emotions related to the original event. Bremner (2002) noted three major problems connected to atrophy of the hippocampus, a breakdown in memory, consciousness, or identity.

McEwen, et al. (1997) reminds us that stress also decreases *"serotonin 5HTia receptor binding within the hippocampus."* Smith, Makino, Kvetnansky, and Post (1995) explain that neurotrophins such as brain-derived neurotrophic factor (BDNF) may be reduced in the hippocampus by stress. Smith, et al. (1995) states that lesser amounts of BDNF could cause cellular death or atrophy of the hippocampus. Numerous other studies also substantiate the changes in the hippocampus.

Many theorists and therapists believed that hippocampal neurons could not be regrown and the accompanying symptoms would have to be endured. The exciting news on the horizon with all this research is the possibility that the hippocampus can regrow neurons even in adults. In other words, the damage may be reversible, at least for PTSD sufferers who are no longer exposed to the stressful stimulus.

In addition to damaging the hippocampus, prolonged cortisol releases may negatively impact the immune system. The early work of Hans Selye (1956/1976) suggested that this prolonged release produces the most harmful stress effects. Resick (2001) states that clients diagnosed with major depressive disorder or an anxiety disorder have elevated cortisol levels. She explains that *"the continued elevated blood sugar and metabolism spurred by cortisol will have an effect on the immune system because there is a shift away from the synthesis of proteins which are necessary for the immune system."*

Although much research has focused on the hippocampus, other areas are affected during prolonged stress such as the amygdala which sits in front of the hippocampus. It is part of the limbic system in the temporal lobe and plays an important role in emotional behavior, particularly aggressive and fear behaviors. The amygdala assists in memory functions also, as well as in motivation. Le Chapman, et al. (1954), Le Doux (1993), and Davis (1992) have shown that the amygdala regulates fear and other emotional responses, and prolonged traumatic stress affects the ability of the amygdala to recognize a real threat. It evokes an over abundance of the fear response to non-threatening events resulting in a *"startle response"* and a continuing arousal state.

The frontal lobe, another important area of the brain, deserves attention in regard to psychological trauma, since it is highly sensitive to stress. The frontal cortex is occupied with planning, evaluating, organizing, and executing; the frontal lobe is also involved in mood regulation and emotion. The medial prefrontal cortex generates primitive fear reactions and also sorts and sifts real from imaginary threats, so we can respond accurately. In prolonged stress, the medial prefrontal cortex malfunctions and cannot tell us which fears pose a real threat and which do not. This inability sets up an unregulated fear response that keeps PTSD clients in a hypervigilant state.

Horowitz (1999) explains that catecholamine chemistry changes during times of stress. These changes involve neural networks that *"connect the limbic, frontal cortical, basal ganglion, and hypothalamic structures."*

> Disturbances in these networks and regions can disturb arousal control and alter the regulation of emotional responses (as in fright and rage attacks). The amygdala may alter its danger-recognition set points, the hippocampus its memory-encoding properties, and the medial pre-

frontal cortex its abilities to establish or reduce associational connections. Such disturbances may partially explain turbulent shifts in states.

PATTERNS OF TRAUMA

The acceptance of Post-Traumatic Stress Disorder (PTSD) as a legitimate diagnostic criteria in the DSM-III has opened the door for continuing research in the study of human suffering. Controversy exists as to whether or not a psychiatric label is warranted for a condition that is a natural response to a horrific circumstance. Some theorists would prefer that it be classified as Post-Traumatic Stress Syndrome, which would remove it from the category of a mental disorder and there is much legitimacy to that desire. On the other hand, the DSM now provides recognition for a common phenomenon that has always existed but was largely ignored.

Four common forms or patterns of trauma have surfaced, which may or may not meet the DSM criteria for PTSD; however, all would fit under the broad umbrella of traumatic stress. They fall into categories of

1. the unexpected
2. the repetitious expected
3. the non-repetitious expected
4. the expected unexpected

The *unexpected* is often linked to a catastrophic event which probably will not be repeated. These events might include such situations as natural disasters, combat, accidents, or rape. The *repetitious expected* is an anticipated event, such as physical or sexual abuse, which is highly likely to be repeated. Victims, often women and children, may not know the exact time of the next assault but they live in a heightened state of awareness awaiting the next occurrence. The *non-repetitious expected* is a one time or singular event that is trauma-producing, but will not be repeated. The anticipated death of a child or loved one after a lingering debilitating illness, or the ultimate bedridden state of a relative caused by a degenerative disease exemplify the non-repetitious expected. The *"expected unexpected"* typifies a victim who lives in dread of a trauma, knowing that the perpetrator will produce one, yet not knowing what face and form it will take. Some domestic situations would fall into this category. For instance, Marian, an unemployed wife, lives with her abusive husband, Frank, and is cognizant of the likelihood of an attack, yet she doesn't know the nature of the abuse she will experience. Perhaps Frank controls her by using a variety of physical, mental, verbal, emotional, financial, sexual, and spiritual forms of abuse. Marian is continually off balance and can't predict even the nature of the abuse, much less it's timing or frequency of occurrence. This is a *"crazy-making"* relationship and Marian, if she stays, may remain in a partially dissociative state as a survival mechanism. Everyone needs some safe arenas in their lives and relationships, realms in which they feel comfortable and non-threatened. If a person feels safe in most arenas, then that individual may *"shut out"* or dissociate in the difficult ones; in other words the trauma would be compartmentalized. In this case, however, Marian isn't safe physically, mentally, verbally, emotionally, financially, sexually, spiritually, or any other way. She is fully feeling the effects of an ongoing *traumatic relationship*. Health care professionals may sometimes encounter clients with such relationships without identifying them as the true traumatic entity that they are.

In reality, trauma is person-specific and may not fit in any category. What is traumatic to one person may not be traumatic for another. Many varying factors determine what constitutes trauma. Helplessness and victimization are the epitome of trauma, so regulating physiological arousal, acquiring safety, and obtaining some control in life is paramount for all traumatized clients.

CHAPTER TWO

Assessment

Assessment serves as the first step in the development of a treatment plan for suffering clients. Clinicians need to interview, evaluate, and diagnose the specific trauma-related disorder or condition and the severity of it. The following definitions may identify some of the more common trauma-based concerns, and serve as a spring board for further analysis.

CURRENT/PROPOSED DEFINITIONS FOR STRESS-RELATED DISORDERS OR CONDITIONS*

> ***Adjustment disorder***—"a general psychiatric category used for a maladaptive reaction to a stressful situation occurring soon (the criterion usually stated is three months) after the onset of the stressor . . . such disorders are quite common and usually temporary; either the stressor is removed or else the person finds a new mode of adaptation to the situation"
>
> Arthur S. Reber
> *The Penguin Dictionary of Psychology*, 1995

> ***Post-traumatic stress disorder (PTSD)***—a DSM-IV-TR "anxiety disorder that emerges following a psychologically distressing, traumatic event such as a natural disaster, accident, war, rape, or the like. The syndrome includes experiencing the trauma in dreams, recurrent thoughts and images, a kind of psychological numbness with an

---

* As designated, some definitions in this book are from *The Penguin Dictionary of Psychology,* 1995 (Reber) and are reprinted by permission from the Penguin Group (USA) Inc.

accompanying lessening of feeling of involvement with the world about, hypervigilance, and an exaggerated startle response. As a psychiatric diagnosis, the term is not applied until the symptoms have continued for at least a month."

Arthur S. Reber
The Penguin Dictionary of Psychology, 1995

Acute stress disorder—a DSM-IV-TR diagnosis for individuals who demonstrate some PTSD symptoms within a few weeks after being involved with a traumatic event. (PTSD cannot be diagnosed until after one month following the trauma.) It is similar to the DSM criteria for PTSD except that it focuses on dissociative symptoms. The symptoms must last for a minimum of two days and a maximum of four weeks, and occurs within the first four weeks of the trauma.

DESNOS—defined in the DSM-IV-TR as "disorders of extreme stress, not otherwise specified." This diagnosis is not rendered separately without a diagnosis of PTSD. It is a supplemental explanation or addition to PTSD. It is a 'catch-all' category for other conditions not adequately covered in the standard PTSD criteria.

Complex PTSD—a diagnostic criteria originated by Judith L. Herman, M.D. (1992) and deals with a "complex form of posttraumatic stress disorder in survivors of prolonged repeated trauma." These survivors, such as domestic victims, sexual victims, hostages, prisoners of war, concentration camp survivors, or religious cult survivors do not readily fit into the existing criteria for PTSD and require an expanded diagnostic concept.

Generalized anxiety disorder—"characterized by persistent 'free floating' anxiety and a host of unspecific reactions such as trembling, jitteriness, tension, sweating, light headedness, feelings of apprehension, irritability, etc.. The term is only used for functional disorders and not for organic disabilities which can produce similar symptoms. Also called, simply, *anxiety reaction.*"

Arthur S. Reber
The Penguin Dictionary of Psychology, 1995

Panic disorders—"a class of anxiety disorders characterized by recurrent panic attacks. The term is not used in cases where a known organic factor is responsible."

Arthur S. Reber
The Penguin Dictionary of Psychology, 1995

Phobic disorders—a term that is synonymous with phobia, a Greek term for fear and dread. "In standard psychiatric work, a reaction requires several factors before it is properly classified as a phobia. Specifically, the fear must be persistent and intense, there must be a compelling need to flee or avoid the phobic object or situation and the fear must be irrational and not based on sound judgment."

Arthur S. Reber
The Penguin Dictionary of Psychology, 1995

Bereavement—classified as a condition, rather than a mental disorder. The Penguin Dictionary states that bereavement is the "emotional reactions felt following the death of a loved one. A full depressive syndrome is considered normal in such a loss."

Arthur S. Reber
The Penguin Dictionary of Psychology, 1995

A **major depressive episode**—depression "with all of the classic symptoms of anhedonia, sleep disturbances, lethargy, feelings of worthlessness, despondency, morbid thoughts, and, on occasion, suicide attempts." The symptoms must exist for at least two weeks before this diagnosis is rendered.

Arthur S. Reber
The Penguin Dictionary of Psychology, 1995

Prolonged grief disorder—a proposed criteria developed by Holly Prigerson, et al. (2007) that may be included as an anxiety disorder in the next DSM. It is a severe psychological wounding caused by a significant loss. The symptoms must be marked and persistent for six months before the diagnosis can be made. This grief leaves the realm of normalcy, and would be classified as a mental disorder.

Holly Prigerson, et al., 2007
American Psychological Association Press

Dissociative identity disorder (DID)—an extreme reaction to trauma where the personality splits and fragments to the degree that pronounced character changes and behaviors are observed. This disorder was formerly called Multiple Personality Disorder.

Dissociative disorder—"a general cover term for those psychological disorders characterized by a breakdown in the usual integrated functions of consciousness, perception of self, and sensory/motor behavior. Generally included here are depersonalization disorder, multiple personality and some forms of amnesia and fugue."

Arthur S. Reber
The Penguin Dictionary of Psychology, 1995

Dissociation—"**1.** Used generally to characterize the process (or its result) whereby a coordinated set of activities, thoughts, attitudes, or emotions becomes separated from the rest of the person's personality and functions independently. Mild forms are seen in compartmentalization, in which one set of life's activities are separated from others, and in the amnesias of hypnosis and some emotional disorders. More extreme forms are observed in the dissociative disorders. **2.** H.S. Sullivan used the term to characterize the process whereby thoughts or memories that produce anxiety are cut off from consciousness. This dissociative reaction (as it is often called) is to be distinguished from schizophrenia on the grounds that each of the dissociated aspects maintains its integrity; one does not observe the general disintegration and loss of contact with reality of the true schizophrenias."

Arthur S. Reber
The Penguin Dictionary of Psychology, 1995

Brief psychotic disorder—"an acute psychotic disorder with the defining feature that the duration is of no more than two weeks. The diagnosis is made when the individual showed normal adaptive functioning prior to onset and when the episode was precipitated by an identifiable and serious psychologically stressful event. Also called brief reactive psychosis."

Arthur S. Reber
The Penguin Dictionary of Psychology, 1995

Depersonalization—"**1.** The dominant meaning is that of the existentialists, who used the term to characterize the feeling of loss of self or of personal identity, the sense that one is but a number in a computer memory bank or mere cog in a blundering, dehumanized, social machine. **2.** In psychiatric terms, it represents an emotional disorder in which there is a loss of contact with one's own personal reality, a derealization accompanied by feelings of strangeness and an unreality of experience. In severe cases, parts of one's body feel alien or altered in size and one may have the experience of perceiving oneself from a distance. To differentiate meaning 1, which does not connote pathology, from meaning 2, which does, the terms depersonalization disorder or depersonalization neurosis are often used for 2. Compare with dissociation, which is a more general term."

Arthur S. Reber
The Penguin Dictionary of Psychology, 1995

Compulsive personality disorder—"A personality disorder characterized by compulsive behaviors, e.g., excessive frugality, obstinacy, cleanliness, etc.. Also called anankastic personality."

Arthur S. Reber
The Penguin Dictionary of Psychology, 1995

Borderline personality disorder—"a personality disorder in which the individual lives 'on the borderline' between normal adaptive functioning and real psychic disability . . . interpersonal relations tend to be unstable, affect shifts dramatically and inappropriately, self-image may be disturbed, displays of anger and temper are common, impulsive acts which are self damaging like gambling or shoplifting are frequent, boredom can become endemic, etc.."

Arthur S. Reber
The Penguin Dictionary of Psychology, 1995

Substance-induced disorders—"an umbrella term for any organic mental disorder that is intimately related to excessive and/or chronic consumption of a substance that has direct effects on the central nervous system. Most commonly these disorders are caused by psychoactive drugs taken nonmedically to alter mood or behavior, e.g., alcohol, barbiturates, amphetamines, cannabis, opiates, cocaine, etc.."

Arthur S. Reber
The Penguin Dictionary of Psychology, 1995

Somatization disorders—"a somatoform disorder characterized by a history of recurrent and multiple physical symptoms for which there are no apparent physical causes. Common complaints are vague pains, allergic, gastrointestinal problems, psychosexual symptoms, palpitations, and conversion symptoms."

Arthur S. Reber
The Penguin Dictionary of Psychology, 1995

Eating disorders—a general term used to cover a variety of conditions characterized by serious disturbances in eating habits and appetitive behaviors, e.g., anorexia nervosa, bulimia nervosa, pica, and rumination disorder of infancy.

Arthur S. Reber
The Penguin Dictionary of Psychology, 1995

Traumatic neurosis—"loosely, any neurosis that develops as a result of some dramatic event such as severe fright, sudden serious injury, and the like."

Arthur S. Reber
The Penguin Dictionary of Psychology, 1995

Derealization—an alteration in the perception of the environment with the sense that somehow one has lost contact with external reality.

Arthur S. Reber
The Penguin Dictionary of Psychology, 1995

THE TRAUMA MEMBRANE

There is much debate in the field of traumatology regarding early interventions. In physiological trauma we know that a quick intervention is often needed to save a life, and minutes can make a difference between life or death outcomes. Very rarely would an early intervention cause difficulty in such emergency situations;

however, psychological trauma operates within a different set of rules. Early therapeutic interventions could retraumatize a victim if pursued prior to the stabilization of the client. The Hippocratic oath *"do no harm"* applies to both the physiological and psychological arenas. Lindy (1996) reminds clinicians that with some trauma, it is a normal adaptation for survivors to use denial and forgetting. They are simply buying time by setting the issue aside. It will be dealt with in small doses as the client is able to bear it. Raphael and Wilson (2000) believe that these emergency defenses may be correlated with the helpful release of neuro-hormones.

If clients are viewed as resistant or in denial, issues that need delay may be forced to the surface, and could cause damage. Lindy and Wilson (2001) explain that the metaphorical *"trauma membrane"* protects the person from an overload of remembering. It is defined as *"the sealing off of traumatic experiences as an adaptive process in the initial phase."* Sigmund Freud (1955/1920) was an early spokesperson regarding the severity of trauma and its effect. He explained that *"trauma by definition overwhelms the protective barrier of defenses; it disrupts the stimulus barrier."* Lindy and Wilson (2001) continue to explain that *"it tears a hole in the survivors' belief that they can handle whatever befalls them."*

Horowitz (1999) reminds us that *"talking"* can be helpful right after a disaster, because it promotes understanding and reduces irrational fantasies about why the tragedy occurred. However, each person has a coping style and they don't all review in the same manner. Horowitz (1999) explains,

> some people seek out every bit of information, others need time for 'dosing' to take in one tolerable bit of meaning at a time, and still others need to take some time off for recovery.

Children in particular may handle trauma in bits and pieces. They may talk about it for a few minutes and then run and play. It should not be interpreted as not caring. It is simply a child's way of handling it.

Survivors with trauma-related conditions may make valiant attempts to avoid any stimulus reminders of the horror they experienced. This theoretical trauma membrane assists with their endeavors of avoidance. Lindy (1985) defines and states the purpose of this trauma membrane. It is a

> semi-permeable membrane which covers the space left in the repression barrier by the trauma experiences. It is

designed to keep trauma reminding stimuli out and to let in only stimuli that will soothe the wound.

Clinicians would do well to respect these natural defenses of protection and work in harmony with them, rather than disrupt them. We must bide our time and wait until the traumatized client is stabilized and invites us to walk behind the membrane with them.

THE TRAUMA INTAKE INTERVIEW

M ost assessment and diagnosis of a client occurs during the initial intake interview. Hospitals, clinics, agencies, or organizations generally have their own standard intake interviews that evaluate psychological disturbance.

John Briere (1997) explains that

> In the interview session, the client is typically evaluated for
>
> (a) altered mental status (i.e., for evidence of dementia, confusion, disorientation, delirium, retardation, or other cognitive-organic disturbance);
>
> (b) psychotic symptoms (e.g., hallucinations, delusions, formal thought disorder, negative signs);
>
> (c) evidence of self-injurious or suicidal thoughts and behaviors;
>
> (d) potential danger to others;
>
> (e) mood disturbance (i.e., depression, anxiety);
>
> (f) substance abuse or addiction; and
>
> (g) personality dysfunction.
>
> In combination with other information (e.g., from the client, significant others, and outside agencies), this interview data provides the basis for diagnosis and an intervention plan.

Although the previous elements are essential for accurate diagnosis, they may not be all-inclusive. Briere (1997) provides clinicians with a timely warning,

> If the presenting problem is a posttraumatic reaction, these standard clinical screens may miss important information. When there is a possibility of trauma-related disturbance, the interview should consider investigating the following additional components, if time allows and the client is sufficiently stable.

Symptoms of posttraumatic stress*

- Intrusive symptoms such as flashbacks, nightmares, intrusive thoughts and memories, reliving experiences, distress or physiological reaction to trauma-reminiscent cues
- Avoidant symptoms such as behavioral or cognitive attempts to avoid trauma-reminiscent stimuli, or psychic numbing
- Hyperarousal symptoms such as decreased or restless sleep, muscle tension, irritability, jumpiness, or attention-concentration difficulties

Dissociative responses

- Depersonalization or derealization
- Fugue states
- 'Spacing out' or cognitive disengagement
- Trance states
- Amnesia or missing time
- Identity alteration

Somatic disturbance

- Conversion reactions (e.g., paralysis, anesthesia, blindness, deafness)
- Somatization
- Psychogenic pain (e.g., pelvic pain, chronic pain)

Sexual disturbance

- Sexual distress (including sexual dysfunction)
- Sexual fears and conflicts

Trauma-related cognitive disturbance

- Low self-esteem
- Helplessness
- Hopelessness
- Overvalued ideas regarding the level of danger in the environment
- Idealization of perpetrators

---

* Reprinted with permission from Psychological Assessment of Adult Posttraumatic States. Washington, D.C. American Psychological Association, 1997.

Tension-reduction activities (Briere, 1992a)

- Self-mutilation
- Bingeing-purging
- Dysfunctional sexual behavior (including sex 'addiction')
- Compulsive stealing
- Impulsive violent behavior

Transient post-traumatic psychotic reactions

- Stress-induced cognitive slippage, loosened associations
- Stress-induced hallucinations (often trauma congruent)
- Stress-induced delusions (often trauma congruent, especially paranoia.)"

In addition to those areas, no assessment is complete without evaluating the impact of losses in life and their accompanying grief. The following list may be useful in the interview process to ensure that adequate attention has been given to grief-related concerns.

LOSS/GRIEF INVENTORY

COMMON FACTORS THAT COMPLICATE GRIEF AND TRAUMA RESOLUTION

Emotional

- Unexpressed hostility
- Prolonged duration of grief
- Delayed and insufficient responses
- Excessive and disabling reactions
- Repressed emotions or absence of emotion
- Unresolved previous losses
- Concomitant losses

Relational

- Narcissistic relationship
- Overly dependent relationship
- Child abuse or childhood trauma
- Insecure childhood attachments

- Death of a child
- Ambivalent relationship with deceased
- Death following a lingering illness
- Uncertain death or missing in action (MIAs)
- Holding onto false hopes
- Sudden unexpected death or loss

Personal

- Self blame for abuse issues
- History of depressive illness
- Personality factors
- Self concept roles
- Belief that loss was avoidable
- Social problems

THE INTER-RELATEDNESS OF GRIEF AND TRAUMA

Although the focus of this publication resides in the field of traumatology, we cannot overlook the inter-relatedness between grief and trauma. It behooves clinicians to reconsider the artificial boundary lines between what has traditionally been viewed as two distinct fields of traumatology and grief. The two fields are more intimately acquainted than originally believed. Bereavement professionals, thanatologists, and traumatologists use the word *"grief"* to describe either an emotion or a process. The use of grief in either fashion connects it to a loss. A few definitions are worthy of consideration.

> Intense emotional suffering caused by loss, disaster, etc., acute sorrow, deep sadness.
>
> David B. Guralnik
> *Webster's New World Dictionary*, 1970

> An intense emotional state associated with the loss of someone (or something) with whom (or which) one has had a deep bond. Not used as a synonym for depression.
>
> Arthur S. Reber
> *The Penguin Dictionary of Psychology*, 1995

"Grief is an intense set of emotional reactions in response
to a real, imagined, or anticipated loss."

Linda J. Schupp
Is There Life After Loss, 1992

Loss is the prerequisite for grief and the entrance into its
domain. When we view grief as real, imagined, or anticipated losses,
then its pervasiveness and impact is clearly seen.

> *Real*—a recognizable event, existing or happening as a
> fact. Example: death, car accident, tragedy.

> *Imagined*—a picture, pretense, assumption, or fantasy of
> what might have been. Example: the normal potential of a
> physically or mentally handicapped child, the monetary
> investment payoff, the promised but undelivered career
> promotion.

> *Anticipated*—looking ahead, predicting, expecting, or
> preparing oneself for an impending loss. Example: terminal
> illness, divorce, loved ones who are missing in action.

Linda J. Schupp, 2003

Although most research and clinical interventions have focused
on the loss of a loved one, the significance and importance of any
type of real, imagined, or anticipated loss is person specific and all
encompassing.

Common Losses		
Loved Ones	Animal companions	Dreams
Marriage	Amputation of body part	Meaning in life
Career	Potential of self or others	Confidence
Home	Image	Faith
Health	Safety	Love
Appearance	Security	Dignity
Mobility	Finances	Identity
Status	Material Possessions	Life style

Linda J. Schupp, 2003

Given this foundation of loss as the etiology of grief, we can conclude that

a person may experience grief without trauma, but you cannot experience trauma without grief.

Early researchers in the study of grief and trauma such as E. Lindemann and A. Adler, who worked with survivors of the Coconut Grove fire in Boston, Massachusetts, can provide us with some observations regarding the interrelatedness of grief and trauma. Lindemann (1944) counseled, studied, and wrote about the normal and abnormal grief reactions of the survivors of the fire while working at the Massachusetts General Hospital. The subject and impact of grief had been given very little recognition until Lindemann published his study in 1944 on *Symptomatology and Management of Acute Grief.* His work paved the way for further studies on the effects of grief. Adler (1943) also worked with bereaved survivors in the emergency room of the Boston City Hospital just across town from Lindemann. She appears to be the first individual to write about the effects of trauma on grieving. In her opinion, it wasn't just the death and loss of a loved one that caused distress, but the horrific circumstances of the death must also be considered.

Therese Rando (1993), a respected researcher and later contributor in both grief and trauma, indicates that there are six primary factors which contribute to a traumatic death.

1. Suddenness and lack of anticipation
2. Violence, mutilation, and destruction
3. Preventability and/or randomness
4. Loss of a child
5. Multiple deaths
6. Survivors personal encounter with death secondary to either a significant threat to survival or a massive and/or shocking configuration with the death and mutilation of others.

Adler (1943) viewed the trauma itself as the most difficult aspect of the loss. Her paper *Neuropsychiatric complications in victims of Boston's Coconut Grove disaster* began the research on traumatic distress. Even today, grief hasn't been fully identified as the traumatic stressor that it truly is, but concepts are changing and grief is increasingly being elevated in its importance.

From those roots, many studies have come forth, culminating in the inclusion of a diagnosis of Post-Traumatic Stress Disorder in the Diagnostic and Statistical Manual of Mental Disorders III in 1980. Finally, a trauma-related disorder had been officially recognized and accepted as a legitimate diagnosis. The PTSD diagnosis is only the tip of the iceberg however; there is much more on the horizon such as the possible inclusion of the Holly Prigerson, et al. (2007) consensus criteria for Prolonged Grief Disorder (PGD) which may become a new entity in the next DSM. This diagnosis will be rendered when there is an extreme psychological wounding that results from any significant loss. As previously indicated, all death-related trauma will be accompanied by grief, so it is an essential consideration for of that type of trauma.

Grief at this time is excluded from significant diagnoses in the DSM-IV-TR and hasn't received a mental disorder recognition. If the Prolonged Grief Disorder criteria becomes a part of the next DSM, the true impact of severe grief will be identified and it is highly likely that clinicians will frequently diagnose Prolonged Grief Disorder as a co-morbid diagnosis with PTSD.

It is indeed curious that the current criteria of PTSD doesn't include grief or even depression as an element of its diagnostic process. Can you imagine the survivors of the September 11th World Trade Centers tragedy *not* suffering intense grief as a part of that horrific experience? Yet, at the moment, there is no accepted official diagnosis that recognizes the extremity and intensity of their grief. This anomaly continues as a subject of much debate, and research is on-going that hopefully will settle these issues.

The forerunners of this integrated approach of traumatology and grief do agree however as to the order in which treatment is accomplished. Trauma issues must be dealt with first prior to grief counseling. The client must be stabilized before beginning to evaluate the enormity of the loss, otherwise the psyche may be overwhelmed and the person retraumatized. Clinicians must respect the *"trauma membrane"* in these cases and handle elements as the client is able to bear it.

With the uniting of the two fields, clinicians must glean from both areas to equip themselves for the days ahead. Since trauma and grief co-exist as a hand-in-glove entity, clinicians must exhibit proficiency in both disciplines if survivors are to be adequately served.

FOUR SIGNIFICANT TRAUMA-RELATED CRITERIA

There are four criteria that are currently in use as diagnostic instruments for PTSD or related symptoms.

1. Post-traumatic Stress Disorder DSM-IV-TR
2. Acute Stress Disorder—DSM-IV-TR

3. Proposed Criteria for Prolonged Grief Disorder
   Holly Prigerson, et al. (2007)
4. Complex Post-traumatic Stress Disorder
   Judith Herman (1992)

All clinicians are aware that both PTSD and ASD are anxiety disorders that are part of the DSM-IV-TR criteria, thus providing them with official recognition and acceptance. It is relatively easy to diagnose PTSD and ASD with the stated criteria for those disorders; however, those criteria fall short in capturing all the elements of Complex PTSD. Judith Herman's (1992) Complex PTSD is commonly used and accepted particularly for clients with repeated prolonged abuse. Holly Prigerson, et al. (2007) proposed consensus criteria for Prolonged Grief Disorder has been receiving recognition and is being used as well. As previously mentioned, it is currently under consideration for inclusion in the DSM-V. Clinicians need to familiarize themselves with these four criteria for a more thorough and accurate diagnosis.

POST-TRAUMATIC STRESS DISORDER
DSM-IV-TR*

A. The person has been exposed to a traumatic event in which both of the following were present:

(1) the person experienced, witnessed, or was confronted with an event or events that involved actual or threatened death or serious injury, or a threat to the physical integrity of self or others.

(2) the person's response involved intense fear, helplessness, or horror. **Note:** In children, this may be expressed instead by disorganized or agitated behavior.

B. The traumatic event is persistently re-experienced in one (or more) of the following ways:

(1) recurrent and intrusive distressing recollections of the event, including images, thoughts, or perceptions. **Note:**

---

* Reprinted with permission from the *Diagnostic and Statistical Manual of Mental Disorders, Fourth Edition,* Text Revision. Washington, D.C. American Psychiatric Association, 2000.

In young children, repetitive play may occur in which themes or aspects of the trauma are expressed.

(2) recurrent distressing dreams of the event. **Note:** in children, there may be frightening dreams without recognizable content.

(3) acting or feeling as if the traumatic event were recurring (includes a sense of reliving the experience, illusions, hallucinations, and dissociative flashback episodes, including those that occur on awakening or when intoxicated). **Note:** In young children, trauma-specific re-enactment may occur.

(4) intense psychological distress at exposure to internal or external cues that symbolize or resemble an aspect of the traumatic event.

(5) physiological reactivity on exposure to internal or external cues that symbolize or resemble an aspect of the traumatic event.

C. Persistent avoidance of stimuli associated with the trauma and numbing of general responsiveness (not present before the trauma), as indicated by three (or more) of the following:

(1) efforts to avoid thoughts, feelings, or conversations associated with the trauma

(2) efforts to avoid activities, places, or people that arouse recollections of the trauma

(3) inability to recall an important aspect of the trauma

(4) markedly diminished interest or participation in significant activities

(5) feeling of detachment or estrangement from others

(6) restricted range of affect (e.g., unable to have loving feelings)

(7) sense of foreshortened future (e.g., does not expect to have a career, marriage, children, or a normal life span).

D. Persistent symptoms of increased arousal (not present before the trauma), as indicated by two (or more) of the following:

(1) difficulty falling or staying asleep

(2) irritability or outbursts of anger

(3) difficulty concentrating

(4) hypervigilance

(5) exaggerated startle response

E. Duration of the disturbance (symptoms in criteria B, C, and D) is longer than one month.

F. The disturbance causes clinically significant distress or impairment in social, occupational, or other important areas of functioning.

Specify if:

Acute: if duration of symptoms is less than three months.

Chronic: if duration of symptoms is three months or more.

Specify if:

With Delayed Onset: if onset of symptoms is at least six months after the stressor.

There are numerous instruments that assess PTSD, either for trauma in a broad sense, or for specific traumas such as child abuse, torture, rape, or combat experiences. The Structured Clinical Interview (SCID) contains the most popular PTSD module that covers a broad range of populations. Although it is excellent for diagnostic purposes, it does not assist in monitoring the progress in symptom change. Many researchers and therapists adhere to the excellence of the Clinician Administered PTSD Scale (CAPS), which serves as a diagnostic tool for PTSD, and measures/monitors the severity of symptoms and the accompanying progress. The Composite International Diagnostic Interview (CIDI) contains a PTSD module which has been used extensively, particularly for research purposes. It can be used by lay personnel as well as clinicians.

It can be beneficial to use a multimodal assessment process. For instance, a client may be hesitant to reveal the full impact of the trauma to a clinician. A self report scale such as the Potential Stressful Experiences Inventory (PSEI) may obtain information that wouldn't easily be shared with the clinician. This scale assesses lifetime experiences of both high and low stressors and focuses on a broad range of traumatic events. By using a variety of instruments, clinicians can more competently and adequately render an accurate diagnosis.

ACUTE STRESS DISORDER
DSM-IV-TR*

Acute stress disorder entered the DSM-IV as an additional entity so that clinicians can provide an early diagnosis during the first month following a trauma and to acknowledge the severity of these symptoms. The symptoms must last at least two days and not more than four weeks. Essentially, it uses the same DSM-IV criteria as for Post-traumatic Stress Disorder, except the person only needs to experience one symptom from each of the PTSD clusters of reexperiencing, avoidance, and hyperarousal. After the initial month, clients should be reevaluated to determine if their symptoms would warrant the diagnosis of PTSD. In ASD, there is greater emphasis on dissociation and three dissociative symptoms must be present for a diagnosis of ASD. A client doesn't have to experience dissociative symptoms for a diagnosis of PTSD, but they must exhibit them for a diagnosis of ASD. The following five DSM-IV-TR dissociative symptoms are used to evaluate ASD:

(1) a subjective sense of numbing, detachment, or absence of emotional responsiveness

(2) a reduction in awareness of his or her surroundings (e.g., 'being in a daze')

(3) derealization

(4) depersonalization

(5) dissociative amnesia (i.e., inability to recall an important aspect of the trauma)"

Although testing may not always be possible or needed in the immediate days and weeks following a trauma, the Acute Stress Reaction Questionnaire (ASRQ) is a reliable instrument that focuses on assessing dissociative symptoms and intrusion, avoidance, and arousal. This instrument could assist clinicians that desire clear distinctions between ASD and PTSD.

Holly Prigerson, et al. (1995)(1997)(2007) met with specialists in fields of trauma and bereavement, and as a group, it was decided that an additional disorder should be proposed for inclusion in the next DSM. They decided on the name Prolonged Grief Disorder for this entity.

---

* Reprinted with permission from the *Diagnostic and Statistical Manual of Mental Disorders, Fourth Edition,* Text Revision. Washington, D.C. American Psychiatric Association, 2000.

PROLONGED GRIEF DISORDER
Proposed Criteria for DSM-V

*DR. HOLLY PRIGERSON, 2007**

Criterion A: Bereavement

1. The reaction has to follow a significant loss.

Criterion B: Separation Distress

The bereaved person must experience at least 1 of 3 separation distress symptoms, such as:

1. Intrusive thoughts related to the deceased.
2. Intense pangs of separation distress.
3. Distressingly long yearnings for that which was lost.

Criterion C: Cognitive, Emotional and Behavioral Symptoms

The bereaved person must experience 5 of the following 9 symptoms daily or to an intense or disruptive degree:

1. Feeling emotionally numb.
2. Feeling stunned or shocked.
3. Feeling that life is meaningless.
4. Confusion about one's role in life, or diminished sense of self.
5. Mistrust of others.
6. Difficulty accepting the loss.
7. Avoidance of the reality of the loss.
8. Bitterness over the loss.
9. Difficulty moving on with life.

Criterion D: Duration

Symptomatic disturbance must endure at least six months.

---

* Reprinted and adapted with permission from Prigerson, H.G.; Vanderwerker, L.C.; Maciejewski, P.K. Prolonged Grief Disorder: Inclusion in DSM Complicated Grief as a Mental disorder: Inclusion in DSM. Chapter 8 in *Handbook of Bereavement Research and Practice: 21st Century Perspectives,* Eds., Margaret Stroebe, Robert Hansson, Henk Schut & Wolfgang Strobe, Washington, D.C.: American Psychological Association Press, 2007

Criterion E: Impairment

It must cause clinically significant distress or impairment in social, occupational, or other important areas of functioning that represents a decrement from the person's normal (e.g., pre-loss) level of functioning.

The PGD criteria is only a sample of what may be submitted to the DSM-V. It can be changed prior to submission or as a requirement for inclusion in the DSM-V.

Dr. Prigerson (2007) explains the timing as to when a diagnosis of PGD can be made and the types of losses that could cause PGD.

> The criteria for PDG proposed for inclusion in the *DSM-V* specify that the particular symptomatic distress must persist for at least 6 consecutive months, regardless of when those 6 months occur in relation to the loss. Hence, chronic and delayed subtypes of grief could both fit within this conceptualization of PGD, as long as the chronicity and delay each include at least 6 months of symptomatic distress. More commonly, however, people diagnosed with PGd do not experience delays in the onset of symptoms post-loss. It is much more often the case among those struggling with PGD that their grief has been intense and unrelenting since the death. Although the criteria we propose here were tested for bereavement, because grief is a response to the loss of something cherished, the criteria may well apply to other significant losses apart from death (e.g., divorce, loss of pets, terminal illness). Future research will need to validate the performance of the proposed criteria with respect to these other types of losses.

In addition to the standard criteria for PTSD, ASD, and the proposed criteria for Prolonged Grief Disorder, Judith Herman (1992) postulates that particular groups of trauma survivors should be diagnosed with Complex Post Traumatic Stress Disorder (Complex PTSD), as opposed to possessing a comorbid diagnosis with a different disorder. Victims of Complex PTSD do not accurately meet the standard criteria for a diagnosis of PTSD because Complex PTSD is symptomatic of a broader range of disorders which sometimes imitate a personality disorder. As an example, Herman believes that repeated violence such as sexual abuse in childhood frequently sets the victim in a position of receiving a diagnosis of borderline personality disorder. It is well documented that the majority of clients with that diagnosis have suffered from sexual child abuse. Resick (2001) also reminds us that any of the classic symptoms of border-line personality disorder such as unstable interpersonal relation-ships, impulsive and potentially self-damaging behaviors, intense reactive moods or inappropriate anger, paranoid ideation, or dissoci-ation could all have their roots in traumatic memories that create difficulties in coping.

The current diagnostic criteria of PTSD has its roots in such traumatic events as combat, natural disasters, bombings, terrorist attacks, car accidents, rapes, shootings, and other horrific circum-stances which leave the survivor with feelings of horror and power-lessness. These disastrous circumstances are certainly characteristic of PTSD and warrant our attention and concern, however, the occur-rence is usually a one time event which is highly unlikely to be repeated in the survivor's life. Lenore Terr (1994) classifies the one time event as Trauma I and multiple events as Trauma II. In con-trast to a singular event, the PTSD criteria may not grasp the total-ity of the complexity of prolonged repeated trauma. Judith Herman (1992) identifies three problem areas of multiple trauma which exceed the diagnostic criteria of classic PTSD.

> The first is symptomatic: the symptom picture in survivors of prolonged trauma often appears to be more complex, dif-fuse, and tenacious than in simple PTSD. The second is characterological: survivors of prolonged abuse develop personality changes, including deformations of relatedness and identity. The third area involves the survivor's vulner-ability to repeated harm, both self-inflicted and at the hands of others.

Herman (1992) has observed three categories that do not follow some of the more classically observed PTSD criteria. They are the *"somatic, dissociative, and affective sequelae of prolonged trauma."* The somatic and affective conditions are nearly always present, but dissociation is also common and may be an essential survival skill, which assists in coping with the unthinkable and unbearable. Hilberman (1980) states that hypervigilance, anxiety, and agitation are earmarks for the chronically traumatized person. Herman (1992) lists other somatic symptoms:

> tension headaches, gastrointestinal disturbances, and abdominal, back, or pelvic pain are extremely common.

Survivors also frequently complain of tremors, choking sensations, or nausea.

Bessel van der Kolk (1996) in a DSM-IV Field Trial demonstrated that the majority of people seeking treatment for trauma-related problems have histories of multiple traumas. These problems include:

Separation and loss
Neglect
Physical abuse
Emotional abuse
Witnessing violence
Familial substance abuse
Other traumas

Dr. van der Kolk states that the individuals with multiple traumas often expressed symptoms such as depression, outbursts of anger, self-destructive behavior, and feelings of shame, self blame, and distrust which caused them to seek treatment, rather than the classic PTSD symptoms.

It has become clear over the years that in clinical settings, the majority of trauma patients present with problems that are <u>NOT</u> included in the PTSD diagnosis. Bessel van der Kolk explains that other clinics included problems with

> depression and self-hatred, dissociation and depersonalization, aggressive behavior against self and others, problems with intimacy, and impairment in the capacity to experience pleasure, satisfaction and fun.

COMPLEX POST-TRAUMATIC STRESS DISORDER*

JUDITH HERMAN, M.D. 1992

1. A history of subjection to totalitarian control over a prolonged period (months to years). Examples include: hostages, prisoners of war, concentration-camp survivors, and survivors of some religious cults. Examples also include those subjected to

---

* Reprinted with permission from the Perseus Books Group, New York, Trauma and Recovery 1992, Judith Herman.

totalitarian systems in sexual and domestic life, including survivors of domestic battering, childhood physical or sexual abuse and organized sexual exploitation.

2. Alterations in affect regulation, including

   - persistent dysphoria
   - chronic suicidal preoccupation
   - self-injury
   - explosive or extremely inhibited anger (may alternate)
   - compulsive or extremely inhibited sexuality (may alternate)

3. Alterations in consciousness, including

   - amnesia or hyperamnesia for traumatic events
   - transient dissociative episodes
   - depersonalization/derealization
   - reliving experiences, either in the form of intrusive posttraumatic stress disorder symptoms or in ruminative preoccupation

4. Alterations in self-perception, including

   - sense of helplessness or paralysis of initiative
   - shame, guilt, and self-blame
   - sense of defilement or stigma
   - sense of complete difference from others (may include specialness, utter aloneness, belief no other person can understand, or nonhuman identity)

5. Alterations in perception of perpetrator, including

   - preoccupation with relationship with perpetrator (includes preoccupation with revenge)
   - unrealistic attribution of total power to perpetrator (caution: victim's assessment of power realities may be more realistic than clinician's)
   - idealization or paradoxical gratitude
   - sense of special or supernatural relationship
   - acceptance of belief system or rationalizations of perpetrator

6. Alterations in relations with others, including

- isolation and withdrawal
- disruption in intimate relationships
- repeated search for rescuer (may alternate with isolation and withdrawal)
- persistent distrust
- repeated failure of self-protection

7. Alterations in systems of meaning

- loss of sustaining faith
- sense of hopelessness and despair

A clinical instrument such as the Early Trauma Inventory (ETI) can be useful in assessing physical, emotional, and sexual abuse in childhood, as well as other traumas. The Child Abuse and Trauma Scale, a self-report assessment, focuses on frequency and intensity of different types of traumatic events from early childhood through adolescence. The Abusive Behavior Inventory (ABI) is a reliable instrument that assesses a wide range of domestic violence abuse. The Combat Exposure Scale (CES) assists in diagnosing war/combat trauma with numerous veteran populations, and the Women's Wartime Stressor Scale (WWSS) focuses on the female experiences of women veterans as well as the sexual trauma and nursing aspects of the war. These instruments concentrate on repeated long term exposure which Judith Herman has labeled Complex Post-Traumatic Stress.

It is essential to query clients regarding the symptoms listed in the DSM-IV-TR for PTSD and ASD, the Proposed Criteria for Prolonged Grief Disorder, and Herman's criteria for Complex PTSD. Some trauma clients are not properly diagnosed because of an inadequate intake interview, so careful history taking is essential. In addition to interviews, diagnostic instruments, and self report tests, a clinician may want to use the Loss/Grief Inventory, van der Kolk's DSM-IV Field Trial list, and the PTSD Predictor's list. Clinicians must also evaluate for co-morbidity of disorders, since PTSD and other trauma-related syndromes rarely travel alone.

Numerous disorders or conditions may present themselves in a disguised fashion. Much diagnostic inaccuracy occurs if a clinician doesn't assess for trauma-related issues underlying the presenting problem. Some researchers have suggested that the following disorders may be trauma-based conditions, at least in a percentage of cases.

DIAGNOSTIC CONFUSION RELATED TO TRAUMA

Some theorists and researchers believe that trauma plays an important role in the etiology of numerous psychopathologies. The following sample of disorders are worthy of consideration as trauma-based conditions.

- Personality disorders, i.e. antisocial, borderline, histrionic, and narcissistic
- Eating disorders
- Conduct disorder
- Obsessive-compulsive disorder
- Substance abuse
- Somatization disorder
- Learning disabilities
- Dissociative identity disorder
- Severely emotionally disturbed
- Malingering
- Affective disorders
- Schizophrenia
- Panic disorders
- Bipolar disorder
- Attention deficit disorder/attention deficit hyperactivity disorder

When we consider the possibility of trauma as the possible etiology for a variety of other disorders, then it brings a whole new perspective and understanding to our diagnostic assessment. How many clients have been misdiagnosed or inadequately diagnosed because a trauma background was overlooked. Sometimes a client isn't responding to treatment because the diagnosis was incomplete and pertinent issues were not addressed. A competent clinician will always look underneath the presenting problem to uncover the hidden vestiges of trauma.

CHAPTER THREE

Treatment Issues and Experiences in Traumatic Stress

T rauma survivors with differing diagnoses will experience trau- matic stress symptoms in a variety of categories. A client does- n't need to be diagnosed with PTSD in order to manifest symptoms that are part of the DSM-IV-TR criteria. It is also important to remember that clients may demonstrate traumatic stress symptoms not covered in the DSM criteria. Clients may express mild, moder- ate, or severe symptomatology, and clinicians need to evaluate the broad range of possibilities that present themselves as traumatic stress reactions.

RE-EXPERIENCING

T he symptoms of re-experiencing are a *"red flag"* in the initial assessment of PTSD since they are distinctive in nature. They are manifested in Criterion B, DSM-IV-TR.

1. recurrent and intrusive distressing recollections of the event, including images, thoughts, or perceptions. **Note:** In young children, repetitive play may occur in which themes or aspects of the trauma are expressed.

2. recurrent distressing dreams of the event. **Note:** in children, there may be frightening dreams without recognizable content.

3. acting or feeling as if the traumatic event were recurring (includes a sense of reliving the experience, illusions, hallucinations, and dissociative flashback episodes, including those that occur on awakening or when intoxicated). **Note:** In young children, trauma-specific re-enactment may occur.

4. intense psychological distress at exposure to internal or external cues that symbolize or resemble an aspect of the traumatic event.

5. physiological reactivity on exposure to internal or external cues that symbolize or resemble an aspect of the traumatic event.

A client needs to experience only one of these symptoms to meet Criterion B of the DSM-IV-TR. Recurrent and intrusive, distressing recollections of the event bombard the person with their unwelcome and undesired content, often becoming so powerful that the person can think of little else. Vivid images, sensations, and feelings are ever present, and the person has a sense of reliving the experience, in the form of illusions, hallucinations, and flashbacks, as well as nightmares related to the event. Any reminder cues, internally or externally, set the person up for physiological and psychological distress. Clients may temporarily lose touch with reality and experience a dissociative state where they respond as though they were actually reliving the traumatic event.

Francine was the mother of two children, Tommy, age eight and Jo Anne, age six. Francine and her husband, Carl, decided to send the children to a well-respected summer camp which began a few days before they embarked on a cruise to the Caribbean. On the second day of camp, the children were playing by a fast moving stream used for river rafting and Jo Anne got too close to the water. She slipped on the mossy bank, and fell into the swirling water where her head hit a large rock, knocking her unconscious. Tommy witnessed this scene, ran downstream, jumped in the fast moving water and frantically tried to reach his sister. His attempts failed and she drowned.

Tommy has experienced frightening dreams, nearly all related to events around water. In everyday life he was visibly frightened whenever an activity required him to be around creeks, ponds, lakes, waterfalls, swimming pools, or any accumulation of water. Even his playtime is reminiscent of his rescue attempts with his sister. When playing soldiers, he frequently sends the troops on rescue missions, perhaps to find an injured or missing soldier. When watching television, he gets agitated if the hero can't rescue the dying victim. It is easy to see that Tommy may have developed PTSD, if he fulfills the additional criterion.

Even though Francine was absent when Jo Anne drowned, she has created vivid images of the horrific event in her mind and is bothered by them during the day. She has experienced nightmares of her little girl crashing against the rock, drowning, then continuing to be carried downstream. She has intense feelings surrounding Tommy's attempts to rescue Jo Anne and has fantasized what that experience must have felt like for him. After the funeral, a friend suggested to Francine that it might be helpful to get away for a while, perhaps taking the cruise that was intended to be her second honeymoon. Francine was angry at the friend's lack of sensitivity but she also became aware of a new sensation. What had been previously viewed as a pleasant event was now seen as extremely distressing, and even thinking about being surrounded by all that water brought intense physiological and psychological distress. Although only one of the five symptoms is required for Criterion B, both Tommy and Francine have several of each, and if the additional DSM criterion is met, then they both will suffer with PTSD. Even without a diagnosis of PTSD, they are experiencing a traumatic stress reaction.

AVOIDANCE

Avoidance of stimuli associated with the trauma and numbing of general responsiveness are the essence of Criterion C of the DSM-IV-TR. A person must experience three of the following seven symptoms:

1. efforts to avoid thoughts, feelings, or conversations associated with the trauma.
2. efforts to avoid activities, places, or people that arouse recollections of the trauma
3. inability to recall an important aspect of the trauma
4. markedly diminished interest or participation in significant activities
5. feeling of detachment or estrangement from others
6. restricted range of affect (e.g., unable to have loving feelings)
7. sense of a foreshortened future (e.g., does not expect to have a career, marriage, children, or a normal life span)

When one has experienced a trauma that is violent, unspeakable, or horrific, it is natural to seek protection both from the memories of the current event and from potential harm of a like or similar event. Most theorists agree that withdrawing from life, isolation of the self, and avoidance of acute reminders are self protective measures. Trauma survivors instinctively know that their physiological and psychological resources have been depleted, and they need decreased stimulation and increased rest and renewal. Just like a wounded animal retreats from normal activities to lick its wounds and heal, the trauma victim seeks respite from the now overwhelming daily burdens of life.

Some amount of avoidance is required to function in life. For instance, Richard can't focus on his son's tragic death which occurred on a climbing expedition at the same time he is conducting a business meeting. Jane cannot think about her assault and rape while teaching an adult education class. Common sense applies here, as to when, where, and how much a person avoids. Temporary avoidance for constructive reasons is healthy, total continued avoidance is unhealthy.

Barbara was on her way to meet her friend Louise for dinner when a man grabbed her on a street corner, thrust a gun in her side, took her to a deserted alley way and raped her. Fortunately, the rapist heard approaching footsteps and ran away. Barbara pulled herself together and went home. She never filed a police report or told her husband Ted about the rape. Almost immediately Barbara became disinterested in sex and couldn't verbally express her love for Ted as she normally did. She stopped socializing with important friends, stating that she needed to spend more time at home. She especially avoided her friend Louise, since she was a significant reminder of the rape. Barbara demonstrates classic symptoms of avoidance and numbing. These defensive measures are attempts to block the awareness and pain of the experience. Barbara may even avoid counseling since she would have to talk about the event. Fortunately for Barbara, her husband Ted saw such an unwelcome, dramatic change in his previously loving and expressive wife, that he insisted on counseling which brought the problem to the light. If Barbara exhibited only the symptoms of Criterion C, she would have a trauma-based condition, not PTSD. However, if she experienced the designated criterion in the other clusters as well, it would then constitute a diagnosis of PTSD.

A common method of avoiding extreme pain in traumatic circumstances is that of psychic numbing, and it is perhaps the most common form of responses to traumatic events. Lifton and Olson

(1976), after working with survivors of the Buffalo Creek flood, describe it as a

> diminished capacity for feeling of all kinds - in the form of various manifestations of apathy, withdrawal, depression, and overall constriction in living . . . That state was a defense against feeling the full impact of the overwhelming death immersion . . . Numbing, then, is an aspect of persistent grief; of the 'half-life' defined by loss, guilt, and close at times to an almost literal identification with the dead.

Grief theorists and therapists tell us that numbing is a *"kissing cousin"* to denial, which frequently accompanies a significant loss in one's life. Denial serves as a protection against the overwhelming acceptance of an enormous loss and could be likened to a form of *"emotional anesthesia."* The unconscious rationale of denial may be, *"if the event isn't real, then I don't have to deal with it."*

Numbing is a form of dissociation and it also depletes energy reserves. It takes much energy to suppress emotions. Fear that the emotion might be too overwhelming can cause a person to numb or dissociate. The attempt here is to block undesirable emotions, but as in a major depressive episode, a client cannot just block the traumatic pain, they numb all emotions, positive or negative. Williams, M. B., & Poijula, S. (2002) list the detrimental impact of numbing the emotions in their PTSD Workbook.*

1. blunted emotional and physical pain, pleasure, and responsiveness; loss of interest in the world and things that previously brought pleasure to you.
2. inability to discriminate between pain and pleasure (when you do not feel emotions, it is easier for you to be revictimized)
3. poor memory; clouded thinking
4. lack of emotional responsiveness leading to feelings of shame and the belief that one is shameful
5. increased need for stimulants and stimulation in order to feel alive; tendency to take risks of all kinds to create excitement and counteract the dead feeling inside you
6. self-mutilating as a way to feel alive
7. episodes of panic and rage

---

8. retreating from life
9. letting your emotional and physical reactions guide you
10. feeling detached from others
11. being unable to experience life because you feel empty inside
12. having no interest in sex; having sexual dysfunction
13. having no energy; feeling apathetic (not caring) and lethargic (being tired all the time)
14. experiencing mental sluggishness

Dissociation provides a distancing step that serves as a defense mechanism. If clients mentally step outside the realms of the trauma, then they aren't as close to it and it doesn't hurt as much. Clinicians will frequently observe their clients using denial and dissociation to soothe the pain.

Sometimes dissociative symptoms appear similar to psychotic episodes and disorders. It is relatively easy to differentiate between dissociative symptomatology and psychotic symptomatology. If a client's narrative descriptions, visual or auditory hallucinations, or olfactory senses are related *only* to the trauma, it would not be considered a psychosis. Familiarity of any form with the trauma is indicative of a person suffering from PTSD. With a psychosis, there is usually no familiarity with the content. The patient may hear a strange voice or visualize a bizarre scene, but it doesn't have to be reminiscent of the trauma. Relatedness to the trauma becomes a key element for diagnosing dissociative symptomatology and distinguishing it from a psychotic episode.

AROUSAL

Increased arousal caused by the overly charged physiological system, is section D of the PTSD criteria in the DSM-IV-TR. This section lists five symptoms as evidence of increased arousal, two of which must be present for the diagnosis. These symptoms manifest as

- Problems in falling asleep or staying asleep
- Expressing irritability or outbursts of anger
- Difficulty in concentrating
- Hypervigilance
- Exaggerated startle response.

Bob came to counseling with a presenting problem of insomnia because his lack of sleep was affecting his concentration on the job. He feared that his inadequate performance would cost him his career if he didn't improve. In reviewing his loss and trauma history, it was discovered that his wife, Jeanne, had been killed by a drunk driver whose out of control car drove onto the sidewalk where she was standing. Every time Bob would walk several blocks to his favorite restaurant, he would jump at the slightest sound of an accelerated engine and he was always looking over his shoulder. In the office, Bob seemed on edge and snapped at his secretary over trivial annoyances. He repeatedly asked her the same questions about business matters, and couldn't remember what she told him.

In Bob's case, he demonstrated all five of the increased arousal symptoms, even though only two were required for a diagnosis of Criterion D. If Bob had experienced only Criterion D symptoms, he would not have met the full criterion for PTSD, but he definitely experienced a trauma-related condition.

Increased arousal symptoms are protective measures designed to prevent another tragic circumstance. This type of anxiety carries with it a sense of imminent danger or impending doom, even when no threat exists.

Alcohol and substance abuse commonly exists as an attempt to calm the increased arousal symptoms and clients should be monitored carefully in that regard. Clients should also be cautioned regarding the use of sympathomimetics. They should minimize their intake of caffeine, chocolate, tea, or soft drinks since those items stimulate the sympathetic nervous system. Sympathomimetics would aggravate an already overly aroused system.

OBSESSIVE BEHAVIORS AND COMPULSIVE RE-EXPOSURE

Traumatized individuals may feel compelled to relive their current or earlier trauma with obsessive behaviors. Judith Herman (1992) reminds us that children often re-enact the scenes of the traumatic event through repetitive actions, and this compulsion is most visible with them through their play. They repeat, repeat, and repeat the trauma in such a manner that it is usually easy to interpret it's meaning. Frequently children will provide a creative or better ending to the trauma.

Herman (1992) further explains that adults may experience the same compulsion to re-create the present or past terror in a disguised form or a literal way. Individuals may unrealistically fantasize that they can alter the end result, but in actuality, they may place themselves in a precarious position of further harm. An underlying motivation exists which desires to overcome the effects of the trauma, and that desire can create compulsive behaviors and reexposure.

Debra, a dedicated employee, was experiencing high levels of arousal after the unexpected death of her sister, and defiantly refused an assignment at work. Subsequently, her supervisor threatened her with suspension and Debra submitted her resignation. The manager of her office recommended counseling and in that safe environment Debra became aware that the abused child within her was resisting the sexual perpetrator of earlier years, and it was a re-enactment of that event. As an adult, she could now exert her power of refusal and walk away from the relationship, even though it could have been damaging in the current situation. Debra commented about the sense of power she experienced when she asserted herself and took care of her needs. Fortunately, her supervisor didn't accept the resignation. Had he done so, it would have placed her in dire financial straits and added additional suffering to the traumatic death of her sister. In this example, the common denominator or trigger for Debra's resignation was the underlying feeling of helplessness. The sudden death of her sister brought those helpless feelings to the forefront and Debra unknowingly responded to her supervisor as though he was the childhood perpetrator.

Margaret, a frail, middle-aged woman, had been robbed and beaten in a dark alleyway of a dangerous neighborhood, yet repeatedly insisted that she wanted to revisit the same place at the identical time of night when she was assaulted. This was her consciously chosen desire which, fortunately for Margaret, her clear thinking family and friends prohibited from happening. She felt she would be obtaining some type of victory or mastery if she could revisit the location alone and not be hurt. Revisitation could be a positive experience and is known as an *"in vivo"* technique, however, the stipulations of this therapy would dictate that the revisitation was accomplished at a safe time of day and with the proper support of protective people. Margaret's method of visiting alone in the darkness would fall into an excessive risk category rather than therapy.

Excessive risk-taking can be a complication of traumatic stress. Bremner (2002) tells us that changes in fear response systems in PTSD patients underlie the ability to correctly identify threat, as if excessive temperatures have broken a thermometer and it can no longer measure the true temperature. This means that trauma clients may place themselves in precarious positions without anticipating the harm that could befall them.

Other researchers have different opinions as to the risk taking factor in trauma clients. Some believe that re-exposure to reminders of the traumatic event can be attempts at mastery, a method to remove themselves from a victim status. For instance, a woman who was sexually abused as a child may thrust herself into questionable relationships.

Clients would greatly benefit from therapists advance warning as to the obsessive behavioral urges that operate consciously and unconsciously. Psychoeducation can serve as preventative therapy for trauma survivors that are prone to obsessive behaviors and compulsive re-exposure.

ENERGY SHIFT

In PTSD or traumatic stress, a major shift occurs where the physical, mental, and emotional energies invested in everyday living are diverted into conscious or unconscious activities. Avoidance is one such example of an energy shift. The energy invested in normal daily affairs is now displaced as the client expends great amounts of energy in avoiding the memories of the trauma. In conversation they try not to talk about it, and in general, they avoid people, places, and objects of familiarity. Often clients are unaware of the enormous investment of energy that is required for avoidance.

The concept of *"trauma bubbles"* was originated by M. Katherine Hudgins (2002) as part of her therapeutic spiral technique. It is a graphic image developed as a shorthand symbol to use with clients to describe the experience of cut-off dissociated trauma material held in unconscious awareness. She states that

> trauma bubbles are encapsulated spheres of active psychological awareness that contain unprocessed experiences. These experiences are dissociated and split off from conscious awareness. Like bubbles, they can be popped unexpectedly, pouring images, sensations, sounds, smells, and tastes into awareness without words.

Tremendous energy reserves are required to keep unprocessed material out of conscious awareness and clients frequently find themselves in a depleted state.

Psychoeducation can assist and provide clients with tools to gradually deal with the trauma. The work of Pennebaker and Campbell (2000) discovered that clients who attempt to suppress the intrusions of images, thoughts, dreams, and memories wind up experiencing more threatening and more frequent intrusions that extend beyond the actual trauma and may contain such content as dreadful events, death, illness, aggression, or failure.

If all physical, mental, and emotional energy resides in unprocessed material, then processing the trauma in doses that are appropriate for the client is the answer in how to shift the energies to the present. An excellent tool for therapists to employ is the *"energy shift"* question. It monitors the client's progress by percentages, and both therapist and client benefit from the information. The client responds to the following question.

TRACK THE TRAUMA

*"How much of my time, energies, and efforts
are involved with the trauma?"*

Clients may respond with 90–95% investment at the onset of therapy which lets the therapist know that little or no processing has occurred. As clients continue to respond to the question, or to *"track the trauma"* the percentages should decrease. Of course the implied question is of equal importance.

*"How much of my time, energies, and efforts
are available for the present?"*

This tracking method assists the client in knowing they are making progress; they need the encouragement or the signposts of healing movement. The question also allows the therapist to know if the current therapies are working and moving the client to resolution.

EMOTIONAL REPERCUSSIONS

Trauma clients often have great fear that the emotions they may experience will be overwhelming and incapacitating. As a result of this fear, they may avoid any stimuli that would arouse these emotions. This client doesn't want to talk about the traumatic event, and may be misclassified in therapy as resistant, when in reality the individual is employing a defense mechanism. If clients avoid thinking and processing, they may feel better temporarily, even though they are lengthening the healing process. Expressing the emotions, regardless of their intensity, is essential and therapeutic, while avoidance will continue the PTSD or traumatic stress symptoms. Clients may also be tempted to turn to drugs and alcohol in an attempt to numb the feelings, which again lengthens the process by avoidance. As mentioned earlier, clinicians need to watch for signs of substance abuse which frequently accompanies intense emotional experiences.

If a client was abused as a child, then she or he may have developed Dissociative Identity Disorder (DID), Borderline Personality Disorder (BPD), or a myriad of other disorders mentioned earlier. There may be excessive mood swings with intense reactions. They may use risky methods of shutting down their feelings such as fast driving or promiscuity. They may view a *"mole hill"* as a mountain and the little irritants of life may become a crisis. Self mutilation and suicide attempts may be a way of dealing with overwhelming emotions.

Other types of emotional repercussions are observed in the early work of Robert Jay Lifton and Eric Olson, (1976). They both worked with survivors of the Buffalo Creek, West Virginia flood disaster and observed that images and memories of the horror were still vivid two and a half years after the event; these were indelible images that threatened to be permanent.

Some trauma survivors will suffer from what Lifton and Olson (1976) termed *"death imprint"* and *"death anxiety."* The death imprint *"consists of memories and images of the disaster, invariably associated with death, dying, and mass destruction."*

Lifton and Olson explain that *death anxiety* characterizes itself when *what was "unnatural" becomes "natural."* In other words survivors expect other loved ones to die; a little stimulus such as rain in their case set up this pattern of expectations. The death anxiety was also manifested through terrifying dreams where the survivor was struggling to remain alive.

"Death guilt" was also present in that survivors condemned themselves for living while others had died. Connected to this guilt may be the failure of the survivor to save the deceased. Anger at self as well as at others who are perceived at fault is also common. These survivors are always searching for the answers to the *"unanswerable question,"* *"Why did I survive and my loved ones died?"*

Since trauma memories are accompanied by intense emotions, survivors may plan their lives in ways that avoid such intrusion. Researchers van der Kolk and Ducey (1989) state that drugs or alcohol temporarily numbs awareness as does dissociation which blocks conscious awareness. Clients need to learn to use physiological techniques such as meditation, breathing, and relaxation to restore their depleted resources rather than self destructive measures. Medication is often required as well.

INFORMATION PROCESSING

Trauma survivors experience internal stress and turmoil, frequently unconsciously, and it restricts their ability to process information. Though they need to attend to present day responsibilities, their energies may be absorbed by areas of unprocessed trauma. One evidence of unprocessed memories is the experience of amnesia. Henry Krystal (1968) examined some Holocaust survivors and explained that *"no trace of registration of any kind is left in the psyche; instead, a void, a hole, is found."* It is no wonder that survivors experience sights and sensations in the present, yet as van der Kolk and Fisler (1995) have stated, there is no way the survivor can make sense out of what they are feeling or seeing. Since much cognitive and emotional energy is absorbed with the unprocessed material, very little energy is available for the tasks of ordinary living.

The term *"biased perception"* has been used by van der Kolk and Ducey (1989) and McFarlane, Weber, and Clark (1993) to explain that trauma survivors react

> preferentially to trauma related triggers at the expense of being able to attend to other perceptions. As a consequence, they have smaller repertoires of neutral or pleasurable internal and environmental sensations that could be restitutive and gratifying.

Some intrusive elements of trauma may be easy to identify at first, but as van der Kolk (1996) reminds us, they may become increasingly more subtle and expand to more generalized areas. He explains that *"what should be irrelevant stimuli may become reminders of the trauma."*

Roger's supervisor is a controlling hyperactive man and in his haste, he often gives confusing and sometimes conflicting instructions. Roger calmly questions and clarifies the supposed contradictions and has been able to perform satisfactorily in this environment for 15 years. He loves his job, as well as his co-workers. Unfortunately, Roger's brother, Harold, became ill and during the course of his treatment in the hospital, he was given a drug to which he had a known allergic reaction. The hospital nurse had duly recorded the drugs to which he was allergic, but the illegible notes were somewhat blurred and obscure. Since the drug in question was usually prescribed for his condition, it was administered to Harold and he died from an extreme allergic reaction. Roger took two weeks off from work, and after that time he thought he could resume his duties. He decided that returning to work would present some sense of normalcy in his life. At least, his days were unchanged and he anticipated his work as therapeutic. However, the resumption of his duties did not turn out as expected. Although everyone was caring and supportive, Roger became increasingly tense, nervous, and irritated with his supervisor and co-workers. Only when he worked with a trauma specialist was he able to view his supervisor's lack of clarity, precision, and accuracy as a stimulus of the *"confused"* prescription that caused his brother's untimely death. In fact, Roger had generalized the *"confusion"* stimulus to everyone he knew. He couldn't tolerate the least bit of confusion and began to withdraw from other co-workers, thus minimizing the occurrence of any confusion. In therapy, the unconscious became conscious, which greatly disempowered his accompanying responses and need to isolate.

Trauma survivors have memories that operate differently from normal memories which consist of verbal sequential processing. Frequently the memories are encoded, pictorially without the assistance of words. The client may not be able to find words to express the horror of the experience. Judith Herman (1992) states that

> traumatic memories lack verbal narrative and context; rather, they are encoded in the form of vivid sensations and images . . . in their absence of verbal narrative, traumatic memories resemble the memories of young children.

Most children under two and one-half years of age cannot verbalize traumatic events, yet they are indelibly encoded in memory (Herman, 1992).

Bessel A. van der Kolk and Alexander C. McFarlane (1996) have summarized the six critical issues concerning information processing with PTSD sufferers.

(1) Persistent intrusive trauma memories which interferes with attentiveness to incoming information

(2) Compulsive exposure to situational reminders of the trauma

(3) Specific avoidance of trauma related emotions and generalized numbing of responsiveness

(4) Inability to modulate physiological responses to generalized stress

(5) Problems with attention distractibility and stimulus discrimination

(6) Alterations in psychological defense mechanisms and in personal identity which changes their perception as to what new information is relevant.*

THE FRAGMENTATION OF THE SELF

Arthur S. Reber (1995) in *The Penguin Dictionary of Psychology* explains the self as follows:

> One of the more dominant aspects of human experience is the compelling sense of one's unique existence, what philosophers have traditionally called the issue of personal identity or of the self.

There are additional amplified versions of the self that are also noteworthy in this psychology dictionary.

1. Self as inner agent or force with controlling and directing functions over motives, fear, needs, etc.

2. Self as inner witness to events.

3. Self as the totality of personal experience and expression, self as living being.

4. Self as synthesis, self as an organized personalized whole.

5. Self as consciousness, awareness, personal conception, self as identity.

6. Self as abstract goal or end point on some personality dimension.

In trauma, the self may experience various levels of fragmenting, splintering, or shattering. The type of trauma one encounters determines the degree of the damage to the self. For instance, if a

---

* Reprinted with permission from Guilford Publications, New York. Traumatic Stress, Bessel van der Kolk, 1996.

person's trauma has been enacted at the hand of a perpetrator, then the fragmentation will be worse. The more control a perpetrator exhibits over a victim, the more fragmentation the victim will experience. In prolonged repeated abuse, the perpetrator's intent is that of *"breaking"* the victim which means the annihilation of a sense of self. This breaking is also known as *"soul murder."*

Hearst & Moscow (1982) and Lovelace & McGrady (1980) describe the effects of some totalitarian systems be they sexual, domestic, political, religious, or otherwise, and explain that even the victim's name may be removed. In some situations, they may be given a number which provides some record of their existence; in other environments, they are nameless and numberless, reduced to a nonentity status. Lovelace and McGrady (1980) and Timerman (1981) tell us that survivors may refer to themselves as a *"nonhuman life form."* There is a vast difference of self descriptions between the victim of a single acute trauma and a victim of chronic trauma. Herman (1992) indicates the one time victim may say she is *"not herself"* since the occurrence of the trauma, however; the victim of chronic trauma may not believe *that she has a self.* Krystal and Niederland (1968) noted that concentration camp survivors demonstrated numerous changes regarding their personal identity. Most of the survivors indicated they were a different person; however, those who suffered the more extreme forms of abuse stated that they were not a person.

Childhood abuse produces many distortions and alterations of the self. Abused children develop even more complicated versions of an identity crisis than concentration camp survivors. The concentration camp survivors never had the initial trust issues with the perpetrator like the child did. They expected *"the enemy to be the enemy."* Quite a different scenario was in place for the child. The very people upon whom the child was dependent, the ones who were supposed to protect and nurture, were the enemy. It is no surprise that numerous psychiatric disorders have their origin in childhood trauma such as Dissociative Identity Disorder (DID) and Borderline Personality Disorder (BPD).

Often the victimized child views the self as ugly, sinful, defiled, contaminated, ruined, or guilty to name a few of the labels of the distorted selves. Although this is a milder form of distortion, it is pervasive and invades all aspects of the survivor's life. We know that beliefs predict behavior, and that a child's perception is his reality, so the lifestyle follows those predictions. Early interventions in children are vital so as to disrupt the formation of damaging beliefs, perceptions, and behaviors.

Horowitz (1999) provides a warning and some advice regarding the impact of traumatic events on identity. Trauma can

> lead to a variety of self concept disturbances such as identity diffusion (a chaotic sense of self fragmentation) or depersonalization. To bolster a sense of identity during stress, an individual often turns for reflectance of self to others. Attachment and bonding impulses are heightened. In such instances, victims may even bond with their aggressors if they are isolated from better sources of support. This can lead to dissociative experiences, in which the aggressor is bad, and in which the aggressor is good. Such segregations of person schematization make it harder to work over and work through memories and fantasies of traumatic events.

Clinicians definitely need to encourage healthy support systems for trauma survivors, as well as being an ideal one. In addition, counselors must watch for dangerous bonding activities with perpetrators, while treating and bringing the client into wholeness.

One of the most extreme forms of fragmentation manifests as Dissociative Identity Disorder (DID), formerly named Multiple Personality Disorder. The American Psychiatric Association changed the name to focus on the identity fragmentation. Bremner (2002) reminds us that it may be a wiser choice to refer to "*identity fragments*" in a client as opposed to separate or multiple personalities. These identity fragments may have been given a name, but they are not complete personalities, they are all part of the person. Putnam, et al. (1986) has shown that nearly all cases of DID are a result of early child abuse. If more resources were channeled into the prevention of child abuse, it would circumvent many of the mental disorders we treat in adults.

In DID the client is frequently in a dissociative state, however, in contrast, the client with BPD never dissociates. Nonetheless, the client with BPD lives on a fine line between normal adaptive functioning and psychic disability.

Herman (1992) points out that persons with BPD possess an unstable sense of self and Kernberg (1967) felt that the splitting of inner representations of self was a dominant feature of this disorder. Herman (1992) reminds us that even though clients with a BPD diagnosis don't dissociate, they do have difficulty in the formation of an integrated identity. Rieker and Carmen (1986) explain the self of abused children as a *"disordered and fragmented identity deriving from accommodations to the judgment of others."* Society definitely needs to invest more resources, time, and efforts into prevention and early treatment of child abuse, and clinicians need to thoroughly evaluate abuse issues when diagnosing children.

CHAPTER FOUR

Physiological Interventions

THE IMPORTANCE OF SLEEP

Harvard psychiatrist and neurophysiologist Allan Hobson (1994) states, *"of all the practices known to be associated with good health, sleep is the most fundamental."* Many PTSD clients report sleep disturbances particularly with nightmares related to the trauma and with heightened arousal symptoms which prohibits the client from falling asleep and staying asleep. Mellman, et al. (1995) and Inman, et al. (1990) have shown that excessive motor activity is also noted while sleeping and when awake indicating the continuous level of arousal in PTSD clients. We know that sleep has restorative value physically, mentally, and emotionally, so lack of it contributes, lengthens, and exacerbates the PTSD condition.

The awakenings during the night may interfere with Rapid Eye Movement (REM) sleep which is known by many theorists to assist in emotional adapting to the traumatic event. REM sleep occurs at regular intervals throughout the night, providing a person with four or five REM cycles in a normal night's sleep. Kramer, et al. (1984) states that most dreaming in non-PTSD clients occurs during the REM cycles; however, nightmares experienced by PTSD clients occur during the REM and non-REM cycles. Mellman, et al. (1995), Ross, et al. (1994) & Kramer, et al. (1984) remind us that if dreams occur in non-REM sleep, they are always preceded by REM sleep.

Psychopharmacology may be indicated in some cases of PTSD. Davidson, et al. (1990) has demonstrated that amitriptyline (Elavil) has a modest effect in suppressing REM cycles and it may be needed on occasion. Armitage, et al. (1994) has proven that nefazodone

(Serzone) is useful in maintaining sleep but it doesn't suppress REM cycles. Clients reported having dreams but they were of a less traumatic nature, however, Reynolds, et al. (1990) reminds us that if REM cycles are suppressed or disrupted, there is increased pressure (reduced latency) for them to return.

REM cycles are an essential component of sleep and if clients are deprived for several nights, the REM cycle will start within a few minutes after sleep begins. In normal sleep, the REM cycle doesn't occur until approximately 90 minutes after the entry to sleep. Some researchers believe that REM is required for organizing information and sorting out emotional ingredients, therefore REM cycles are needed and an essential part of healing. Of course, this is a catch 22. If REM is beneficial, yet prevented, it may delay emotional processing and ultimate healing time. On the other hand, if a client refuses to go to sleep for fear of the nightmares, then progress is also slowed and recovery delayed. These situations require the assistance of competent medical professionals and drugs administered on a case by case basis. A trial-and-error approach must sometimes be applied to assist the client with insomnia.

The best current information we have on treating PTSD symptoms is with selective serotonin reuptake inhibitors (SSRIs). They have proven themselves effective in all three categorical symptom areas, intrusion (increased arousal causing sleep disturbances), re-experiencing (the nightmares), and avoidance. Agreement among professionals on prescribing SSRIs as the first line of treatment is consistent and the studies support these drugs.

Clinicians have known for several years that the release of serotonin and norepinepherine decline steadily across the sleep cycle, thus allowing less depletion of those essential neurotransmitters. One hypothesis is that PTSD symptoms are caused by the depletion of serotonin; therefore the more serotonin in the system, the less PTSD symptoms. Until more research occurs, medical personnel must treat cautiously and carefully and on a client by client basis.

STRESS INOCULATION TRAINING

S tress Inoculation Training (SIT) consists of numerous coping skills that assist in anxiety reduction in the trauma survivors' everyday life. This umbrella can be a catch-all for stress management and the term is frequently used to cover various forms of relaxation, breath work, biofeedback, physiological interventions, role playing, communication techniques, assertiveness training, thought stopping, and various self-regulation techniques. Some of these areas will be covered individually.

RELAXATION

Reber (1995) states that relaxation is

1. Most generally, the state of low tension in which emotional level is diminished, especially the level of emotions such as anxiety, fear, anger, and the like.

2. The process used to bring about this state.

3. More specifically, the return of a contracted muscle to its normal resting state.

The Penguin Dictionary of Psychology, 1995

Reber further defines relaxation therapy:

Generally, any psychotherapy that emphasizes techniques for teaching the client how to relax, to control tensions. The procedure used is based upon E. Jacobson's progressive relaxation techniques in which the individual learns how to relax muscle groups one at a time, the assumption being that muscular relaxation is effective in bringing about emotional relaxation. Jacobson's techniques are often used in various forms of behavior therapy; desensitization procedure.

The Penguin Dictionary of Psychology, 1995

Because of the increased arousal state that exists in many trauma survivors, the need for relaxation has heightened importance. Relaxation is person specific, but it allows trauma survivors to engage themselves in an experience that causes them to temporarily lose track of time. The following guided imagery is a positive form of dissociation that should be encouraged.

A.   Guided Imagery

Guided imagery uses the senses in a creative manner. While listening to an audiotape, a client can visualize himself walking in a forest with pine needles crackling under his feet, smelling the scent of the pine, listening to a babbling brook, or seeing the brilliantly colored flowers beside the pathway. A client may want to make his own relaxation tape using whatever images work best. The familiarity of one's own voice is pleasing to the psyche and offers no resistance to the message. Since trust is a major concern with clients who have been violated by another person, they may not be comfortable allowing another individual to guide their thoughts. In this case, clients may tape their own message, saying exactly what is wanted or needed.

B. Progressive Relaxation

Progressive relaxation is a series of tensing and relaxing various muscle groups. The client may sit comfortably in a chair and start by tensing the muscles in the feet, hold it for a few seconds, then release. They then tense the calves in the legs for a few seconds and release. They continue to work upwards tensing and releasing each muscle group.

Since trauma survivors already feel tense much of the time, it helps them to *"go with the tension."* Accentuating the tension in different muscle groups and then relaxing each group gives them a sense of control or mastery over their physiological condition.

C. Active Relaxation or Recreation

Active relaxation or recreation consists of any activity that temporarily absorbs the client. It could be knitting, crocheting, checkers, chess, puzzles, cards, painting, drawing, playing an instrument, gardening, walking in the park, playing football or basketball, hiking or biking, any pursuit that provides a constructive outlet for the pent-up emotional energy. Trauma survivors already experience an aroused system, so releasing that energy in a healthy way assists in the healing process.

D. Passive Relaxation

There are some trauma survivors who will not participate in active forms of relaxation. They may benefit from something more sedate and less taxing. Passive relaxation is an involvement that requires little expenditure of energy. Perhaps a client might experiment with reading a good book, listening to favorite music, sunning in a backyard lounge chair, or watching favorite movies or television programs.

When a person has experienced a trauma, they may not want to engage in any activities, even ones that were considered previously pleasurable. It is important that they participate in some form of relaxation even if it provides only a small amount of momentary pleasure. Those tiny bits of distraction provide some reprieve from the constancy of focusing on the trauma.

EXERCISE

Under normal circumstances, exercise is widely touted and generates numerous physical and psychological benefits. Much information on the market explains the physiological advantages such as cardiovascular strengthening, lowered blood pressure, reduced pain, mental acuity, and euphoric feelings. One might speculate that exercise would do wonders for clients with PTSD.

Much research such as Sime (1984) clearly specified that exercise can decrease anxiety and depression. Since PTSD is classified as an anxiety disorder, an easy assumption would be to randomly prescribe exercise. Another convincing piece of information comes from Westerlund (1992), who worked with incest survivors, and showed that exercise provided a sense of control over their bodies. We know that PTSD survivors desperately need control on physiological, mental, and emotional levels. As with other forms of self-regulation, some clients may benefit, while others may not. In general, exercise is known to reduce anxiety so aerobics or running is a productive method of releasing the ever present tension that PTSD clients experience. Exercise can serve as an outlet for an increased arousal system.

Jon Allen (1995) reminds us that some clients may find aerobic exercise to be anxiety provoking, and it could be accompanied by a panic attack. Exercise increases arousal initially and a client could associate the feeling of arousal with the trauma. He indicates that clients could experience flashbacks, dissociate, and become confused and disoriented. Obviously, moderation is the key until the client knows what is helpful and what is not.

Anaerobic exercise can also be employed such as weight lifting which uses short bursts of energy, intermittent with rest periods. Some clients found that trauma-related anxiety symptoms were reduced or released by pushing against a heavy object or lifting weights. Perhaps these movements were symbolic or representative of unconscious material. For instance, a woman that was raped might find relief in thrusting a heavy weight away from her body symbolizing an ability to push the attacker away. This exercise could assist in a feeling of mastery or control.

Self-styled exercise such as gardening, walking in a park, sight-seeing, or any activities that keep the client moving at a leisurely pace can assist in the healing process. Often it is helpful for a client to start slow to check their tolerance ability. Not all clients are able to exercise, particularly in a vigorous manner.

On a positive note, Allen (1995) states that exercise can *"provide a sense of predictability, control, and accomplishment. Success is just doing it regularly—at whatever level."*

BREATHWORK

B reathwork is another popular form of relaxation. Since trauma-spectrum clients frequently suffer from increased arousal, it is important for them to gain control and mastery of their body. If breathing exercises are performed correctly, they can assist with anxiety management. However, not everyone can use breathing techniques. For instance, Allen (1995) cautions us that any activity that causes a person to gasp for breath, even though it is unrelated to the trauma, can evoke traumatic memories and cause re-experiencing of the original event. If a client is working hard at accomplishing a particular breathing technique and it brings up memories, obviously another version should be tried and the distressing technique eliminated. This difficulty in relaxation is known as *relaxation-induced anxiety*, and some clients associate relaxation with letting down their guard. In order to be successful, they must be certain they are in a safe place. It is noteworthy that Walter Cannon's fight or flight response which activates the sympathetic nervous system is the exact opposite of the state of relaxation that slows metabolism (Allen, 1995). Some clients could feel vulnerable in such a relaxed state. Others might begin to dissociate or feel spacey. Despite the obstacles to relaxing, the following four techniques have been beneficial to numerous traumatized clients. Often these techniques are used for relaxation before processing traumatic material, as well as for closure of the therapy session.

A. Diaphragmatic Breathing

1. Sit comfortably erect in a chair with feet on the floor. Wear loose clothing which permits ease of breathing.
2. Place hand on diaphragm to ensure proper breathing. (If clients are concerned that they may be experiencing shal-

low breathing, instruct them to lie on their back. It will naturally force them into diaphragmatic breathing.)

3. Inhale slowly through the nostrils filling the diaphragm with oxygen. Then exhale slowly through the nostrils. Nostril breathing is preferred, as opposed to breathing through the mouth, because it stimulates important brain centers.

4. Use this technique several times during the day, as needed, for five to ten minutes.

B. Visualization

To enhance the diaphragmatic breathing, a client may add some form of visualization. Clients are free to choose an image that is helpful to them. For instance, as clients inhale, they might choose to visualize puffy white clouds (symbolizing life giving oxygen) filling the body. As they exhale, they could visualize black smoke (typifying toxins in the body) leaving the system.

Note: If the client's trauma involved a fire, then the smoke image could be retraumatizing. This explains the reason why it is important for clients to choose their own images.

C. Balloon Breathing

1. Stand upright with arms relaxed at sides.

2. Breathe deeply through the nostrils, filling the diaphragm.

3. Hold breath about five seconds while tensing all muscles in the body, particularly neck, shoulders, and upper arms.

4. Consciously become aware of what tension feels like in your body and where it resides. During grief or trauma, some individuals are not aware of how much tension the body is holding, so this purposeful tensing of the muscles accentuates it and brings awareness.

5. After holding breath about five seconds and tensing muscles, release the air suddenly through the mouth. (This resembles popping a balloon.)

Breathing has an important relationship to trauma and grief. Shallow breathing serves as a negative defense function for *cutting off feeling*. When we repress emotions (hold them in) such as fear, anger, or grief, it hinders and short circuits breathing.

Conscious deep breathing assists in expressing and releasing emotions appropriately.

D. Timed Breathing

This is an excellent technique to slow down the breathing process. The increased arousal that trauma clients may experience could cause them to breathe faster than they should. This places them at risk for re-experiencing or dissociation. The therapist may instruct the client in the following simple steps.

1. Therapist asks client to close his eyes.
2. Therapist uses stop watch and asks client to breathe normally and count the breaths sub-vocally.
3. Client inhales and exhales for a minute. Therapist calls the time to stop. (If client breathes 18–22 times a minute, it indicates high anxiety. A relaxed person should breathe 8–12 times a minute.)
4. Client practices counting breaths until he can gain control and lower the number of breaths.

This technique is excellent for physiological control and mastery. The client can then time themselves whenever it is needed. This simple method adds to their repertoire of self-regulation techniques.

SENSORIMOTOR PSYCHOTHERAPY

Sensorimotor psychotherapy was developed by Pat Ogden (2000) and is based on her clinical experience. Ogden states that

> trauma profoundly affects the body and many symptoms of traumatized individuals are somatically based . . . Sensorimotor Psychotherapy is a method that integrates sensorimotor processing with cognitive and emotional processing in the treatment of trauma . . . by using the body (rather than cognition or emotion) as a primary entry point in processing trauma. Sensorimotor Psychotherapy directly treats the effects of trauma on the body which in turn facilitates emotional and cognitive processing.

This process is an excellent supplemental therapy and isn't designed to function alone. Ogden explains, *"The full spectrum of*

Sensorimotor Psychotherapy integrates sensorimotor processing with emotional and cognitive processing."

Ogden cites an example of a woman that had been sexually abused as a child and explains how the therapy would proceed. She asked the client to revisit the trauma and notice the bodily sensations. Since the woman was sexually abused as a child, she begins to re-experience those bodily sensations such as submitting and dissociating from her body, which was evidenced as numbness, muscle flaccidity, and feeling paralyzed. The client simultaneously felt an impulse to fight back which was demonstrated as tension in her jaws and arms. Two different themes were at work and appeared as a *"dissociative split,"* but in therapy, they were easily understood by the client. She was able to recognize that the disintegration wasn't real; in actuality she was experiencing herself as two bodies inside herself expressing two different things. Part of her had to submit and dissociate, and yet another part of her wanted to fight. Understanding this split caused her to heal. It also helped her to accept her dissociation as a way of surviving the horrific abuse.

As part of this therapy, the client is instructed to move the body in any way that it dictates such as hitting, pushing, kicking, or making a fist. The body has a language of its own which needs to be expressed. These bodily expressions may be performed alone or the client can push against the therapist in a non-violent manner.

Special training is offered in Sensorimotor Psychotherapy. Clinicians may contact the Sensorimotor Psychotherapy Institute and Naropa University, Boulder, CO. (www.sensorimotorpsychotherapy.org)

TRAUMA TOUCH THERAPY

Trauma Touch Therapy is a hands-on body-oriented modality which falls in the broad category of massage therapies. It assists the emotionally numb client to feel again. Since the body remembers the trauma on a cellular level, it is important to work with the somatic memories that it is holding. Clients probably wonder why numbing is considered a problem when it seems quite natural for them to not want to feel their pain. The difficulty lies in the fact that the numbing process can't differentiate which portion of the person should be anesthetized, and which should continue to feel. Happiness, energy, and motivation may also be blocked along with painful memories.

Trauma Touch is a slow gentle therapy which integrates the mind and body. Since the body or parts of the body may be temporarily disowned or dissociated, it is essential that they be resurrected and reconnected to the whole. Chris Smith (1993) the founder of Trauma Touch Therapy is a survivor of sexual abuse and understands the need for healthy touch from the personal and professional level. She developed this approach to work with her clients who had been traumatized by domestic violence, childhood abuse, illness or death of a loved one, or any other traumatic event. It generally consists of 10 sessions and the client is in control of the process. Questions are asked such as *"in what part of your body do you feel the pain or tension?" "Describe the pain or tension."* Then the therapist asks permission to touch it, if it is a location that doesn't violate ethical standards. If granted, the gentle touch massage begins. The client is typically clothed and can sit in a chair or lie on the massage table. Smith (1993) doesn't claim that she conducts psychotherapy, although her touch therapy enables emotions to surface. She requires that clients work with a psychotherapist to interpret the meaning of the emotions and doesn't treat clients unless they are in therapy with someone.

Clients tell the Trauma Touch therapist what is needed. Perhaps they simply hold a spot or they gently massage; maybe they simply assume a quiet calming stance. The goal is helping the client to view the body as a safe place, and this goal is realized in baby steps. The therapist must be alert to reading the client's body language as to how the touch is affecting them. Slowly but surely, the client is awakened and the numbness disappears, emotions and memories surface, and healing takes place.

MASSAGE

Massage therapy has become a popular, acceptable stress management technique. The best therapy is performed by a trained massage therapist and requires a certificate through the American Massage Therapy Association. Since a traumatized person may be anxious and in an aroused state, various types of massages may be helpful.

A. Mechanical Shiatsu

Mechanical Shiatsu is a small machine which serves as a powerful massager that can soothe aches and pains and relieve tension. It is convenient to use at home or during breaks at work. It consists of two circulating balls that provide deep tissue pressure on whatever portion of the body is placed between the rotating balls. This technique may work well with clients that are unable to tolerate touch from another person.

B. Acupressure

Acupressure, an ancient Chinese remedy, affirms that energy blockages cause physical, mental, and emotional problems. Many of these problems are relieved by putting pressure on certain locations/points of the body. The pressure points may also be stimulated by acupuncture which uses needles. Some traumatized clients may resist acupuncture, but could benefit from acupressure.

C. Swedish Massage

Swedish massage, the gentlest, most soothing form of massage, requires the trained hands of a massage therapist. Soft lights, scented candles, soothing music, and creamy oils and lotions often accompany the massage. Since traumatized clients frequently experience anxiety and tension, a massage can refresh and relax them for a short period of time before they return to the difficult adjustments they are making in their lives.

Note: Not every client will benefit from massage. Clients such as those who are rape victims or who were physically or sexually abused may be retraumatized by being touched. As with any therapy, it is person-specific and relative to the needs of the client.

MEDITATION

Since recovery from PTSD uses multiple modes of treatments, the basic self care treatment of meditation has its place in the healing process. Regaining some amount of control over the physiological arousal in the body is paramount and mediation assists with that goal. Meditation is defined as a relaxation technique that increases one's ability to focus or concentrate. It assists in producing a calm, relaxed mind. Robert Benson (1975) recommends four elements that are required for relaxation and a meditative process.

1. A quiet environment without distractions and disturbances.

2. A mental device as a focal point such as a visual image or sound.

3. A passive, calm attitude.

4. A comfortable relaxed body position.

In trauma, the client may be experiencing the interruptions of intrusive thoughts and images. *"Exclusive meditation,"* a technique that calms and quiets the mind, assists clients by blocking distracting thoughts, and teaches them to focus on one single object. The client may want to practice concentrating on an image such as a bowl of fruit, a vase of summer flowers, a loved one's face, a glass of ice water, a beautiful mountain scene, a cascading waterfall, or any other image that evokes a peaceful picture. If disturbing thoughts enter, the client can choose to let them pass and exit. The client is instructed to keep the focus on the desired object, holding it as the principal focus of concentration. Clients need to grasp the concept that *"thinking is stressing,"* therefore; any reprieve from thinking of the trauma gives clients some sense of control over intrusive thoughts and images.

St. Francis of Assisi explained that distracting thoughts are like birds flying in the air. You can't stop them from their flight, but they don't have to make a nest in your hair. In like manner, you can't stop distracting thoughts from passing by, but you don't have to focus on them.

A technique called *"not thinking"* is a simple form of meditation. For five or ten minutes, a person can concentrate on a continuous sound such as an air conditioner, heater, a bubbling fish tank, or the client's own breathing. Every time the person drifts into thinking, than a conscious shift must be made to listen, and focus again only on the sound. At first, a traumatized person may only be able to meditate in this manner for a few seconds, but as they practice it, they will be able to *stop thinking* for longer periods of time. With the constant bombardment of thoughts during the aftermath of a traumatic experience, a little rest can be deeply appreciated.

MINDFULNESS

Mindfulness falls under the general category of meditation. This technique uses all the senses in focusing and concentrating exclusively on the activity that one is involved in at the moment. The person is totally present and available to the activity, which could be anything the person is doing; examining the colors and shape of a flower, preparing a dessert, mowing the lawn, or petting a cat.

Why is the practice of mindfulness helpful with a traumatized person? Because mindfulness is the opposite of dissociation and it provides some sense of control in keeping the client in the present. Very little literature exists regarding effective ways to deal with dissociation; however, this technique can assist on certain occasions. For instance, the client could choose some object before processing traumatic material in a counseling session and the object could be called upon if the client begins to dissociate. The client may choose to focus on a flower arrangement in the room, which represents the here and now. If the client dissociates momentarily, a gentle reminder from the therapist such as *focus on the different colors in the flower arrangement* could change the direction of the client's movement and attention.

Dissociation is linked with a sense of non-reality; even the harmless habit of daydreaming can be a mild form of temporary dissociation. Mindfulness keeps us in the here and now by focusing on what we are experiencing in the present, whether that is the simple act of breathing or listening to the hum of the air conditioner. The benefit of this form of therapy lies in its ability to separate the past from the present. As human beings we can truly only live in the present.

VITAMIN AND MINERAL THERAPIES

Traumatic stress is a major stressor, and as such it quickly depletes a person's body of certain vitamins and minerals. The following three vitamins promote mental alertness and assist in overcoming depression and insomnia, all of which can benefit a traumatized client.

1. Vitamin A
2. Vitamin C
3. Vitamin E

These three are considered antioxidants and essential in fighting free radicals. Under normal conditions when the immune system is not under attack, vitamins A, C, and E are able to metabolize free radicals. However, when trauma strikes, Seaward (1999) states these vitamins are depleted and the body may not be able to adequately absorb them. Studies prove that trauma clients are susceptible to coronary heart disease and cancer, and free radicals are associated with those diseases. It is wise to supplement these vitamins during the healing process.

4. B-Vitamin Complex

The B vitamin complex aids the central nervous system which is aroused during and after a traumatic event. Vitamin B6 assists in overcoming depression and increases immune function. *Some experts believe that liquid vitamins or sublinguals are easier to take and have greater absorption in the body.*

Minerals are also important considerations. The stress of trauma depletes certain minerals such as magnesium, copper, iron, zinc, and chromium. This depletion compromises the immune system and renders the traumatized person more susceptible to disease and illness. It would be beneficial for traumatized clients to supplement their diet with these essential minerals.

PSYCHOPHARMACOLOGY

Davidson and van der Kolk (1996) reviewed the psychopharmacological treatment for PTSD and came up with the following goals for the use of such medications.*

(1) Reduction of frequency and/or severity of intrusive symptoms

(2) Reduction in the tendency to interpret incoming stimuli as recurrences of the trauma.

(3) Reduction in conditioned hyperarousal to stimuli reminiscent of the trauma, as well as in generalized hyperarousal.

(4) Reduction in avoidance behavior.

(5) Improvement in depressed mood and numbing.

(6) Reduction in psychotic or dissociative symptoms.

(7) Reduction of impulsive aggression against self and others.

If a medication doesn't serve these purposes, then the need for it should be re-evaluated.

---

* Reprinted with permission from Guilford Publications, New York. Traumatic Stress, Bessel van der Kolk, 1996.

Many medical and psychological professionals are claiming that selective serotonin reuptake inhibitors (SSRIs), such as paroxetine (Paxil), sertraline (Zoloft), fluvoxamine (Luvox), fluoxetine (Prozac), and citalopram (Celexa), are the treatment of choice for PTSD and other trauma-related disorders and conditions. Although not everyone agrees, one hypothesis for a biological basis for PTSD, as well as depression, would be a deficiency of the neurotransmitter serotonin. The benefits of SSRIs have been clearly observed in clinical practice and this class of drugs has outperformed other types in drug trials. SSRIs have proven to assist with such PTSD symptoms as intrusive recollections, avoidance and numbing, and hyperarousal, as well as treating comorbid disorders such as Obsessive-Compulsive Disorder, Major Depressive Disorder, Panic Disorder, and Alcohol Abuse. Research by Friedman (1990) and Brady (1995) have shown that SSRIs are also helpful in regulating PTSD symptoms such as rage, impulsivity, obsessional thinking, and suicidal ideation. The SSRI's beneficial effect is due to their ability to block the presynaptic reuptake of serotonin which leaves more serotonin within the system. The SSRIs have been researched more thoroughly than any other drugs and at this point in time, they are considered the most effective. As brain research expands it's horizons, newer medications may arise.

Bessel van der Kolk, et al. (1994) found that fluoxetine, commonly known as Prozac, when administered at doses of 40 mg. or higher was beneficial in civilian-related PTSD, but not combat-related PTSD. The effectiveness of the medication varies depending on the origins of the PTSD. Brady, et al. (2000) has demonstrated that sertraline (Zoloft) was quite effective in women, with only moderate improvement in men. Gender, then, also affects the performance of the drug.

In addition to gender, age plays a role in regard to the performance of a drug. DeBoer, et al. (1992) has discovered that selective serotonin reuptake inhibitor antidepressants frequently provide better results than benzodiazepine hypnotics when treating symptoms of disturbed sleep and dreaming in elderly trauma victims.

It is believed by many experts that SSRI medications can actually reverse the negative impact that traumatic stress has on the brain. For instance, the work of Bremner (2002) has proven that atrophy occurs in the hippocampus due to increased cortisol. Gould, et al. (1998) found that the hippocampus was capable of *"neurogenesis,"* which means that even in adulthood, new neurons could grow. Serotonin assisted with the reproduction of new brain cells.

Davidson and van der Kolk (1996) recommend SSRIs as the first option for PTSD symptoms, but feel that there may be some clients who can't take them or would benefit from carefully managed benzodiazepines such as alprazolam (Xanax) and clonazepam (Klonopin). These anti-anxiety drugs can reduce anxiety, fear, insomnia, hyperarousal, jumpiness, anger, startle response, and irritability. Resick (2001) states that clonidine (Catapres) and propranolol (Inderal), seem to assist in curbing sympathetic arousal and adrenergic activity. According to Kinzie & Leung (1989), Kolb, Burris, & Griffiths (1984), Perry (1994), these drugs reduce nightmares, intrusive memories, hypervigilance, startle responses, insomnia, and angry outbursts.

Southwick, et al. (1994) has studied the effects of tricyclics, antidepressants, and monoamine oxidase inhibitors (MOI) on PTSD clients and found that they were somewhat effective for re-experiencing symptoms, but not for avoidance and arousal.

Most clinicians today wouldn't diagnose PTSD clients as having a psychotic disorder. If clients experience dissociation, it is linked only to the trauma, not randomly across the board as in a psychotic state. Most of the PTSD symptoms such as agitation, paranoia, impulsivity, dissociation, and hypervigilance can be mitigated by either antidepressants or anti-adrenergic medications. It would only be the occasional client who would require an anti-psychotic drug. Some psychiatrists believe that medications such as risperidone (Risperdal), quetiapine (Seroquel), and olanzapine (Zyprexa) could be considered, but should be administered sparingly since they are relatively new and their effectiveness has not been evaluated extensively.

More extensive research needs to be conducted in the area of anticonvulsants. Carbamazepine (Tegretol) and valproic acid (Depakene) have been prescribed for PTSD patients in small open trials. Friedman & Southwick (1995) have shown that carbamazepine is effective *"in reducing intrusion and arousal symptoms, while valproate has reduced avoidant/numbing and arousal (but not intrusion) symptoms."* Hopefully, research will continue with these drugs and with the newer ones such as lamotrigine (Lamictal) and gabapentin (Neurontin).

Edna Foa, et al. (1999) have shown that a panel of experts recommended SSRIs as the best available treatment in the present. The same group of experts also felt that combination therapies with mood stabilizing agents should be administered. Probably the most important decision regarding the efficacy of SSRIs was the decision by the U.S. Food and Drug Administration to put their stamp of approval on sertraline as a drug to treat PTSD. Sertraline, commonly known as Zoloft, reduced symptoms in all three areas of intrusion, hyperarousal and avoidance/numbing. An interesting side note regarding SSRIs is that they also treat alcoholism and depression which can accompany PTSD. The U.S. Food and Drug Administration based it's decision on two large trials conducted by Brady, et al. (2000) and Davidson, Malik, & Sutherland (1996) where participants received either a placebo or sertraline. Prior to these studies, some researchers seriously wondered if PTSD sufferers would have to take separate drugs for the PTSD symptoms. Therefore, it is good news that sertraline treats all three areas.

CHAPTER FIVE

Treatment Techniques for Trauma

THE RELATIONSHIP AS THERAPY

Trauma survivors have experienced the world as an unsafe place due to unexpected events that have been out of their control. Some have also encountered or lived with people who violated their trust and perpetrated harm against them. Because of their perceived lack of control and misused, misplaced trust, clients may be rightfully suspicious of baring their souls to a stranger that claims to *"help and care."* Because of the fragility of clients' emotions, shattering and retraumatization could easily occur. Counselors must proceed with caution like a skilled surgeon who delicately and deftly uses the correct instrument with accuracy and precision.

With trauma clients, the relationship itself becomes the initial tool. Compassion must be conveyed before competence can be appreciated. Trust must be built and established before facilitation can occur. Until trust is built to some degree, testing for Post Traumatic Stress Disorder or other related traumas may need to be delayed or perhaps eliminated altogether. Since PTSD and trauma-based conditions are easy to diagnose in an informal way, to administer a test to a traumatized client may appear harsh and abrasive. Counselors need to be a person first, professional second.

Every human being has a deep longing and need to be heard and understood. Of all clients, trauma survivors need these elements

81

more than most. Even though the counselor may not have experienced any situation that remotely resembles the trauma of the client, the counselor can use bonding techniques such as Identity Clues. Every client possesses certain traits, mannerisms, characteristics, beliefs, and behaviors that constitute the individuality of that person. The more similar counselors appear to clients, the greater comfort the client will experience. *"Commonalities create comfort; differences produce distance"* (Schupp, 2003). If clients are comfortable, they are more likely to discuss the trauma. If they are afraid the counselor can't handle the pain of their experience, then they may not talk about it. Therefore, it is extremely important to use rapport-building techniques such as the following.

IDENTITY CLUES

1. Agree when possible.

2. Paraphrase or restate their words, experiences, ideas, beliefs, values, feelings, principles.

3. Match their verbal energy.

4. Imitate some of client's body language.

Linda J. Schupp, 2003

The technique of agreement can support the client by providing some commonality and similarities.

Jennifer is the wife of John who worked as a pilot for a large airline. Unfortunately, his plane crashed in a thunderstorm killing him and many passengers. Jennifer came for counseling and in addition to her intense grief, she complained about jumpiness and unwarranted anxiety. Although she didn't recognize it, she was experiencing the *"startle response"* which is common in PTSD. Jennifer told her therapist:

> Every time I hear a truck roaring down the highway, I relive my perception of John's death.

The therapist may choose to respond

> I probably would react just like you if I had been through the same experience.

This statement agrees with the client in a supportive manner, and also validates the normalcy of her reactions. Jennifer's faith has been radically shaken and she poses an unanswerable question to the therapist.

> I prayed to God everyday asking him to protect my husband in his flights as a pilot. Why didn't God answer my prayers?

The counselor, in this case, shares the same faith as Jennifer and responds

> You know, Jennifer, I also pray for protection of my loved ones, and I would be asking the same question if my husband had died in an accident.

The technique of agreement supports the client's feelings and questioning, thus providing an open door for Jennifer to discuss and evaluate her theological beliefs. Trauma deeply touches the spiritual components of the fabric of life and can shatter one's faith at a time when it is most needed. As counselors, we can facilitate the feelings, frustration, questions, and pondering. One of the healing components in trauma is to assist our clients in learning how to live without answers. Those who provide pat answers to the unspeakable horrors that some of our clients experience inflict further damage on that suffering population. Therapists may choose to simply agree in an honest forthright manner whenever possible.

The popular technique of paraphrasing has been titled in many ways such as reflective listening, pacing, mirroring, backtracking, and restating. Whatever label it wears, paraphrasing is the only technique that provides *"proof positive"* that we have truly entered the trauma survivor's world of perception. It may meet some of their most intense therapeutic needs.

To express the inexpressible, to speak the unspeakable, and to know that one has been heard, understood, and validated, is a gift and service that perhaps only a caring counselor can provide. There are numerous reasons for a counselor to paraphrase, however; some are more relevant then others for trauma survivors.

THE NEED TO PARAPHRASE

1. Meets client's deepest needs to be heard and understood.
2. Reveals that counselors are not afraid of client's pain.
3. Encourages clients to express more fully and to continue sharing.

4. Conveys that counselors are connected to clients in their journey.
5. Proves that counselors can handle whatever horrific situations clients need to share.

This technique can also provide counselors with a non-hasty response when they don't know what to say or they need to momentarily regroup.

Let's look at how paraphrasing can meet some of Jennifer's needs in the counseling session. Jennifer is continuing to relive the traumatic untimely death of her husband and expressing thoughts about what John experienced before the airplane crashed.

> How horrible for John when he realized he was going to die. He couldn't protect himself or his passengers. What agony he must have experienced. Perhaps he wondered how his death might affect me and our baby girl.

The counselor could respond with the following paraphrase.

> It must be difficult for you, Jennifer, when you try to figure out what John was thinking, feeling, and experiencing before his death. I'm sure you wonder what his thoughts were in regards to you and the baby. That must have been agonizing for him at that time and it is certainly painful for you at this time.

Paraphrasing in this example captures the essence of what Jennifer is stating, believing, pondering, and feeling and then reflects it in the counselor's own words. With some originality on the counselor's part, it doesn't sound like polly parroting. If the counselor feels that a paraphrase might sound patronizing, then a qualifier could be offered prior to the paraphrase.

> Jennifer, I know how painful it is for you to think about and express your thoughts surrounding the moments before John died, and because our discussion is relevant to your healing, I want to be certain I'm following your thoughts and feelings. If I heard you correctly, . . .

If a counselor uses paraphrasing, the client recognizes that the counselor has walked into her trauma, heard her pain, and understood the situation to the degree possible. If there was ever a time to use paraphrasing, it is with a traumatized client who has allowed a clinician to see inside the gaping wounds of the soul. Counselors can reflect with accuracy, care, and concern that the client has been heard on the deepest level.

Imitating the tone and tempo of the client's voice is another bonding technique that wields an unconscious influence. It is a way of matching their verbal energy. Most traumatized, grieving, or ill clients have very little energy in their voices and they may speak slowly and softly. If so, the counselor can slow her pace and tone to more closely, but not exactly, resemble the client's. The counselor should not imitate the client exactly or the client might perceive it as mockery. If the counselor speaks rapidly or loudly when the client is speaking slowly and softly, then the counselor will appear as a complete opposite and become an irritant. Opposition produces stress and strain in the relationship. Similarities and commonalities help the client relax in the counselor's presence. If the traumatized client picks up the pace and speaks in a more animated fashion, the counselor may speed up also and use more expression.

However, a word of warning is due when imitating the tone and tempo. Do not ever imitate negativity. If a traumatized client suddenly screams at the counselor, the counselor shouldn't return the angry response. Anger only escalates anger. In a case of an angry client, a reflective technique could be used such as: *"If I were in your shoes, I might feel the way you do."* Legitimize the behavior as much as possible. Keep in mind, we don't know exactly how we would feel or act until faced with a similar trauma.

Therapists can also enter the world of the client by using body language, since it encompasses 55% of the way messages are sent. It is a powerful signal which can create feelings of connectedness. Therapists can choose to imitate some of the client's body language.

If the client is intently leaning toward the counselor, the counselor might lean slightly forward to indicate interest in what is being said. If a client leans backward against the couch, the counselor might wait a few moments, and then lean slightly backward without the counselor's body touching the couch. Counselors don't want to look exactly like the client. The intent is to partially imitate. If a counselor imitates the client precisely, or makes a change as soon as he does, it could appear as mockery or patronizing. We don't want the imitation to be obvious. The purpose of the technique is to achieve harmony with the client on as many levels as possible.

Mirroring facial expressions can also be useful. If the client appears sad, and is expressing a downcast look, the counselor certainly doesn't want to reflect happiness and joy. Reflect the client's pain with a serious expression. If a traumatized woman, for instance, begins to smile slightly, you might offer a similar smile. This should not be done in a robot-like fashion, but in a natural way, that allows the counselor to become part of the experience bodily. Mirroring the breathing patterns of the client can also be useful, particularly if the therapist wants to decelerate the breathing of the traumatized client. The therapist can join the client, then guide the client into a slower breathing pattern. The more of these bonding techniques that are used, the more comfort the client experiences and the easier it will be to facilitate the healing process.

COGNITIVE BEHAVIORAL THERAPY (CBT)

Aaron Beck (1976) and Albert Ellis (1962) are attributed with being the most influential pioneers of Cognitive Behavioral Therapy (CBT). Many studies point to the success of this therapy in working with depression, post-traumatic stress disorder, and other trauma-related syndromes. It is a highly regarded treatment for PTSD and some believe it to be the best treatment that is recorded in the current published literature. There are numerous cognitive behavioral techniques which are used separately and in conjunction with each other. Some of the most frequently used techniques are Stress Inoculation Training (SIT), Cognitive Processing Therapy (CPT), Cognitive Therapy, Exposure Therapy, and Systematic Desensitization. Reber (1995) provides us with the following definition:

> An approach to psychotherapy based originally on behavior therapy and consistent with its basic tenets. The novel aspect involves the extension of the modification and relearning procedures to cognitive processes such as imagery, fantasy, thought, self-image, etc.. Proponents of the approach argue, not unpersuasively, that what the client believes about things he or she does and about the reasons for them can be as important as the doing of them.

The theory behind Cognitive Behavioral Therapy draws from the research on learning and conditioning. This theory applies quite naturally to PTSD where client's cognitively recognize and emotionally respond to a life-threatening situation.

The client has learned that a particular situation can be dangerous, and the aroused emotions now alert him or her to other potentially threatening circumstances. The client is conditioned to respond to certain emotional stimuli which then creates the appropriate needed behaviors.

The following model may be helpful in minimizing the painful emotions that result from distorted thinking surrounding a trauma. The premise of this therapeutic model states that *"we can change our feelings by changing our beliefs."*

A. Action

Describe what happened.

B. Beliefs

List the negative messages you are repeating to yourself.
1.
2.
3.

C. Consequences

What emotions are you experiencing regarding the traumatic event?

I feel _____

D. Defense Attorney

Write out your defense against the negative beliefs in B.
1.
2.
3.

Marjorie and Frank were excited that their daughter Patricia was graduating from college and marrying her fiancé Scott. Patricia never seemed happier and her life's dreams were being fulfilled. Marjory and Frank decided to buy her a new car to celebrate these landmarks in life. They also figured that Patty and Scott would have a safe enjoyable vehicle to drive on their honeymoon trip. The wedding was lovely, and after the reception, the young couple began their 200 mile trip to a lovely mountain resort. While traveling in the mountains, they came upon an area of slippery roads caused by a downpour of rain. The car hydroplaned, sped uncontrollably off the road, slid over the side of the mountain, killing them both. The parents both experienced intense grief and trauma as would be expected; however, Frank's pain was deepened even further by distorted thoughts connected to the trauma. The use of the following model assisted Frank in eliminating the painful emotions connected to his distorted thinking.

A. Action

Describe what happened.
My daughter was killed in a car accident.

B. Beliefs

List negative messages you are repeating to yourself.
1. *I am responsible for my daughter's death.*
2. *I should have bought airplane tickets for them.*
3. *I should have bought a better car for them.*

C. Consequences

What emotions are you experiencing regarding the traumatic event?
I feel guilty, devastated, and depressed.

Note: These emotions will assist in diagnosing the severity of the impact of the trauma.

D. Defense Attorney

Write out your defenses against the negative beliefs in B.

Note: The following No. 1, 2, and 3 refute the corresponding numbers 1, 2, and 3 of the Beliefs.

1. *I'm not a mind reader. There's no way I could have known about or prevented this accident.*
2. *They didn't want to fly, because they wanted to sightsee along the way.*
3. *They would have driven an older car with more wear on the tires, if I had not bought the new one.*

Note: When the negative distorted message appears, the client needs to read and re-read the Defense Attorney (DA). Clinicians may request that clients review the facts of the DA a few minutes in the morning, several times during the day and in the evening before retiring. This repetition bombards the distorted thinking and eventually overpowers it. This technique will assist in minimizing the pain of unwarranted emotions.

NON-VERBAL TRAUMA THERAPIES

ART THERAPY

Some pain lies so deep within the unconscious recesses of a traumatized client that words are unable to verbalize it. Art therapy is a multimodal approach that provides clients non-verbal emotional expression which may extract traumatic material that would remain unprocessed. Clients may use such techniques as drawing, painting, sculpting, or molding. Colors, texture, patterns, or movements facilitate with a language of their own.

Bernie Siegel (1986), an ontological surgeon uses art therapy with his cancer patients. His intake interview consists of handing out sheets of white paper and crayons, and asking the patients to draw themselves as they perceive their state of health or illness. Siegel believes the drawings are a better indicator regarding the prognosis of the cancer than other diagnostic instruments. Clinicians may consider asking trauma clients to draw themselves in regard to their mental and emotional health. For some clients without adequate words to express the trauma, this tool could prove useful.

Art forms can be especially helpful with children, particularly younger children that lack verbal skills and vocabulary. They may be asked to draw their feelings, and often deeply repressed emotions can surface on paper, canvas, or clay. Talent is not required and anyone can use art therapy.

Art therapy has been successful in treating PTSD patients who have survived the horror and bloodshed of war. Many soldiers were emotionally distraught by memories of destruction and death when they returned home, yet some didn't want to verbally share their experiences. They found expression for the often unexpressionable in art therapy.

JOURNALING

Journaling opens the door to the conscious and unconscious. It facilitates a healthy expression of perceptions, emotions, reflections, thoughts, conflicts, beliefs, challenges, disappointments, failures, and hopes for the future. Journaling is usually a daily process which keeps a current record of the trauma consequences, emotions, and healing. Because of the frequency of writing, it is easy to track the progress of healing. A backward glance at previous days, weeks, and months compares the past with the present. Trauma victims need encouragement and signposts that are indicative of their progress, so journaling accomplishes that purpose as well as providing self awareness.

WRITING

Writing can take a variety of forms, and is another non-verbal expression which puts words to feelings. Letters can be written to a perpetrator, a deceased loved one, to God or anyone that captivates the myriad of emotions that require release or closure. Letters can express what a person never said or couldn't say, such as apologies, anger, fear, forgiveness, *"I love you"* or *"I hate you."* Many varying and sometimes conflicting emotions need to be facilitated. On occasion, it can be a healthy venture to take on the role of the recipient, and write a return letter from that person. It forces clients out of their own emotional box and may bring some clarity to certain situations.

Another writing exercise is the composition of a narrative of the traumatic event/experience, its impact and the feelings it has generated. A person could donate large amounts of time or shorter amounts to this project. This narrative could be written in a personal fashion in the first person voice, or if distance is required due to the traumatic nature of the event, the client could write it as though it had happened to someone else. This form of writing belongs to a group of desensitization techniques which have proven helpful in PTSD.

POETRY

Some believe that poetry may provide a more in-depth form of facilitation. Certain types of poetry use *"rhyme and rhythm,"* and freely employ metaphors and similes. There is balance, symmetry, and sequence in the cadence of the words. This style of writing may generate a feeling of balance and orderliness at a time when the trauma has stolen a sense of control from the person's life. After the death of my 18 year old son, Cliff, I expressed many of my memories and pain through the vehicle of poetry.

Wilted Roses and Pious Platitudes

Wilted roses and pious platitudes,
    How they harm, and blame, and destroy.
I listened each day as they came and they went;
    And I watched the effects on my boy.

The intent of the folks who offered the words,
  Was certainly good, right, and true.
But I noticed that Cliff was no better off;
  In fact, he seemed wearied and blue.

The comforters, armed with their empty clichés,
  Took aim and went straight for his heart.
They claimed that the Father had given them words,
  Their duty it was to impart.

When they needed to talk, and expound, and advise,
  Cliff listened to all that they said.
Then thanked them for coming, and offering God's words,
  After all . . . they claimed to be led.

They rarely listened to my son,
  Though the thoughts he expressed were quite rare,
But they didn't mind using his limited strength;
  And I questioned: "Do they really care?"

When they asked how he felt and he honestly spoke,
  They suddenly seemed to go deaf.
The subject would change or the interest would shift;
  And frequently, the comforter left.

Then quietly, after the clamor was gone,
  We'd reflect on the message they aired.
And this thought just kept coming and coming again;
  It was really my son who had cared.

"Mom, I know they mean well, but they don't meet my need
  And from them I've got to be free.
My strength is near gone, still I hear what they say;
  But why . . . don't they listen to me?"

Wilted roses and pious platitudes,
How they harm, and blame, and destroy.
To this day I can see and feel their effects;
But they no longer bother my boy!

Dedicated to my son
William Clifford Taylor
Died—Nov. 3, 1978

EYE MOVEMENT DESENSITIZATION
REPROCESSING (EMDR)

Eye Movement Desensitization Reprocessing (EMDR) was developed by Francine Shapiro (1989) from a personal experience while taking a walk. She noticed that disturbing thoughts were calmed when her eyes shifted from left to right and right to left. From this initial observation, she began to use it in her clinical practice with much success. Shapiro (1989/1995) states that EMDR should be classified as accelerated information processing that utilizes bi-lateral stimulation of the brain.

EMDR has more scientific research as a trauma treatment than any other method, except for medications. Shapiro (1998) indicated that EMDR has been used successfully by over 10,000 clinicians trained in it. Figley & Carbonell (1995) obtained data from licensed therapists all across the United States regarding which techniques were most effective for PTSD. Four techniques surfaced.

(a) Traumatic Incident Reduction (TIR)

(b) Visual/Kinesthetic Dissociation (V/RD)

(c) Thought Field Therapy (TFT)

(d) Eye Movement Desensitization Reprocessing (EMDR)

These four techniques were than tested on 51 people who demonstrated trauma-related symptoms. All four treatments were beneficial and produced lasting results. EMDR was listed as first choice, being slightly more effective, and it clearly improved trauma symptoms such as nightmares, intrusive recollections, and phobic responses. Because of its proven track record and its rapid response rate, it is becoming a popular technique. There is debate however as to whether the eye movements are a required ingredient. Other methods such as saccadic ear tones and tapping are also effective. The theory behind the process is still unclear, but the results testify to the effectiveness of the treatment.

Bessel van der Kolk, Burbridge, and Suzuki (1997) conducted an important study using neuroimaging to pinpoint affected brain areas while EMDR is being performed. Their study agrees with Bremner's (2000) study and others regarding decreased hippocampus volume in PTSD clients.

This decreased volume is related to the increased activation of the amygdala, the emotional part of the brain. The hippocampus portion is a *"cognitive map"* and assists in information processing.

Bessel van der Kolk proved that PTSD symptoms were mediated by increased activation of the anterior cingulate and the prefrontal area, which distinguishes between real threats and past trauma cues that are no longer relevant.

Because of the importance of a client's interpretation in regard to healing, EMDR becomes an important technique. The following steps explain the process.

1. A client identifies a traumatic memory and a visual image or picture that accompanies it.

2. A Subjective Units of Distress (SUDs) rating is given by the client on a scale between 0-10, with 0 meaning no disturbance when thinking of or picturing the trauma and 10 being the most disturbance imaginable.

3. The negative cognition (belief) attached to the picture is defined. Ex. "I'm defenseless, I allow people to take advantage of me, I'm worthless, etc.."

4. A positive cognition is explored as to what the client would like to believe regarding the self or the situation. Ex. "I'm able to defend myself." "I'm assertive and I stand up for myself." "I am a worthwhile, valuable person."

5. The client decides how true the positive cognition feels at the moment. It is rated on a scale of 0–7, with 7 being a totally believable statement and 0 being non-believable.

6. The client then tracks the therapist's fingers as they move rapidly from left to right and right to left between a 1¹/₂ to 2 foot space. Each left/right-right/left movement constitutes a set. Approximately 24 sets of eye movements are performed. (Other methods can be used such as a light bar, ear phones, tactile stimulation, and tapping on the client's left and right hands, shoulders, or knees in a rhythmic manner.) At the beginning of the tracking, the client is asked to visualize the traumatic image and repeat the negative cognition. Then the process takes over, and the brain does its own healing. There is no talking during the eye movement time.

7. The therapist stops after the desensitizing eye movements and checks in with the client. "What's happening?" Client gives brief statement, and therapist says, "Stay with that or go with that memory." Then eye movements begin again.

8. After several sets of eye movement, the therapist checks the SUDs rating. It may de-escalate as the disturbance decreases.

Therapist continues eye movements until distress level is at least 1 or 0.

9. The positive cognition is than installed by the client repeating the desired belief to the self and sets of eye movements are continued until the new cognition is at a 6 or 7 believability level.

Shapiro (1998) poses the following explanation for her treatment's success.

> . . . negative life experiences of trauma are those which upset the biochemical balance of the brain's physical information processing system. This imbalance prevents the information processing from proceeding to a state of adaptive resolution with the result that the perceptions, emotions, beliefs, and meanings derived from the experiences are, in effect 'locked' in the nervous system. The EMDR methodology, as a form of Accelerated Information Processing, may unblock the brain's information processing system through a number of ways.

CLIENT DIRECTED EYE MOVEMENT TECHNIQUE

The concept of Subjective Units of Distress (SUDs) must first be understood by the client before proceeding to the technique itself. The SUDs level is a subjective measurement from 0–10 that determines the amount of distress the client is experiencing. The ratings are usually viewed by EMDR specialists as a range of numbers between 0–10 which describes the disturbance of the emotion. The lower numbers 0–1 indicate no distress or minimal distress and the number 10 reveals the highest imaginable distress.

Clients can interpret for themselves the severity of the emotions that fall in between the highest and lowest range. After clients evaluate their level of disturbance, they then visualize a disturbing picture/image or identify a bodily sensation or emotion that represents the distress. While viewing this picture and feeling the bodily or emotional disturbance, they move the eyes rapidly from left to right and right to left. This movement constitutes a set and should take about one second. The client can use from 24 to 30 sets, and the eyes should be open during this process. They can use a range of approximately 1½ to 2 feet apart for the left to right/right to left movement. The corners of a picture frame or perhaps a narrow window could provide a stable spacing. Clients could use their knees as a viewing mark if nothing in the room will work. After the eye movements the client can determine by measuring the SUDs level if some of the distress, anxiety, or emotional pain has decreased; if not, they continue the eye movements until improvement has occurred to the degree possible.

The therapist may use the standard EMDR process of instructing the client to follow the fingers of the therapist in the back and forth procedure as a *"teaching tool."* If the client experiences a decrease in the problem, then they know it will work for them. Clients are then encouraged to use it on their own for symptom control. They can also use it with their eyes closed by shifting eyes from side to side beneath the eyelids. There may be times when it would be embarrassing or inappropriate to use the open eye procedure, yet symptom management is immediately required. Empowerment of this nature is greatly needed by some clients because their loss of control in life has severely disempowered them or placed them in a victim position.

EMOTIONAL FREEDOM TECHNIQUES (EFT)

E motional Freedom Techniques (EFT) designed by Gary Craig (1995) is a therapy with its roots in ancient Chinese Medicine and the modern science of Applied Kinesiology. This therapy uses acupuncture points and the theory that all disease, physical or emotional, comes from blockage in the energy system. Tapping or massaging these points frees up the blockage. EFT teaches a simple recipe which can be applied to a wide variety of problems. Simple phobias are corrected in minutes, depressions lift, anxieties are calmed, and pain is reduced or disappears altogether.

Each year we learn more about how our brain functions. We now know that flashbacks from trauma are a result of over activity in the right brain (amygdyla) and under activity in the left brain (brochus) leading to an inability to make cognitive/behavioral changes in the emotional response to an event from long ago.

Dr. Candace Pert (1997), a research scientist who discovered the receptor sites for opiates in 1972, has continued her research in the area of peptides. Her research shows that peptides have the same capacity for communication, as do the neurotransmitters in the brain. However, peptides reside not only in the brain, but throughout the body and in every organ. She has mapped clusters of peptides in the areas of the body that have been used as acupuncture points for thousands of years. She theorizes that the energy meridians described by the Chinese are actually the pathways used by the peptides to run the immune system in the body. Her research shows the body gives messages to the brain and the brain gives messages to the body with equal authority. She describes this as *"mind-body"* or *"bodymind."* Her explanation puts science behind Applied Kinesiology (muscle testing) and Acupuncture, the two theories used in EFT.

EFT is simple, can be taught to someone in a single session, and does no harm. It does not require specific training in psychology to be used successfully. There are five points on the face, two on the body, and five on the hand. Gary Craig (1995) developed EFT after completing all available training in Thought Field Therapy (TFT). He simplified TFT and formatted his *"Basic Recipe"* so that it can be learned quickly and remembered easily. In addition, this is a tool that can be used in any setting. (Dr. Sheryl Brickner, Article for CoACCT newsletter, 8-3-99).

TAPPING SITES AND SEQUENCE

EB	=	Beginning of the Eyebrow
SE	=	Side of the Eye
UE	=	Under the Eye
UN	=	Under the Nose
Ch	=	Chin (crevice) between lip and chin
CB	=	Beginning of the Collar Bone (1 inch down)
UA	=	Under the Arm (about 6 inches down)
Th	=	Thumb (outside area next to nail)
IF	=	Index Finger (outside area next to nail)
MF	=	Middle Finger (by nail facing index finger)
BF	=	Baby Finger (by nail facing ring finger)
KC	=	Karate Chop (side of hand below baby finger)

Tap each point five-seven times working your way down the face to the collar bone, under the arm, then thumb and fingers. Either left or right side of body can be used for tapping. Focus on the disturbing event, thought, or feeling while tapping the 12 designated points.

This treatment also uses the technique of *"Psychological Reversal."* It is caused by negative self-incriminating thinking and can defeat the effectiveness of the treatment. To reverse a negative effect a person must use a neutralizing affirmation such as *"Even though I can't control my physiological arousal, I deeply and completely accept myself."* The person would repeat the affirmation three times while rubbing the sore spot at the base of the throat where a man would knot his tie, or the client could tap the Karate chop spot, which is the outside portion of the hand below the little finger. This technique clears the energy system and allows the tapping sequence to fulfill its task.

Emotional freedom techniques (EFT) can serve as a supplemental stabilization intervention, particularly in the area of physiological control. EFT is helpful in providing a sense of self control for trauma victims. Since trauma produces helplessness and a feeling of being out of control, any measure of control can be empowering. Because trauma victims may view their body as an out-of-control enemy, the physiological responses need to submit to the survivor's control. As mentioned earlier, survivors administer the tapping sequence to themselves, thus allowing self-regulation of becoming calmer and less disturbed. They can use the SUDs rating system to determine the degree of severity and improvement.

EMDR AND EFT

Some clinicians have found that the combination of EMDR and EFT amplifies the benefits of therapy. EFT appears to supplement and enhance the rapid response rate of EMDR treatment. It also provides physiological control of disturbing body memories. Some proponents of EMDR believe that EMDR therapy can be useful in the reintegration of the fragmented self as well as in resolving the trauma. Since EMDR is accelerated information processing, it is logical to assume that if symptoms of the trauma have been reduced in a few sessions, then personality issues such as the fragmented self, should also show improvement. This improvement in personality problems may occur as a result of a change in the client's worldview. Trauma clients have a distorted view of the world and EMDR provides them with a more realistic one. EFT provides additional physiological stability while EMDR is solving trauma issues and perhaps integrating the shattered fragments of personality.

RESOURCE DEVELOPMENT AND INSTALLATION

A ndrew Leeds (1999) originated Resource Development and Installation and believes that it contributes crucial elements to the treatment of PTSD and other trauma-based conditions. This self-enhancing and strengthening technique enables the client to acquire a more stable ego structure. This technique is frequently used in conjunction with the standard EMDR protocol. Leeds theorizes that positive resources (positive memories) are normally acquired in childhood through nurturing, supportive parents. Children develop healthy self objects relations or self esteem from meaningful relationships with primary care givers. Some clients may not have been privileged to develop these supportive internal systems and they need that inner strengthening before they can work on traumatic memories or they need these resources while processing difficult situations. Otherwise the client may be retraumatized.

A client is asked to identify a quality in the self that needs strengthening, a difficult life circumstance, a belief that needs changing, or a maladaptive schema. The client then thinks of a positive experience with good feelings and brings that affect into the difficult situation, which hopefully assists in minimizing, or offsetting the negative feeling. If a client can't find a positive memory or feeling, they can think of or visualize a powerful person effectively interacting in their negative memory.

Another option is the incorporation of a symbolic representation of the needed resource. For instance, an abused frightened little girl who was frequently locked in a dark closet might imagine that a loving nurturing person was in there with her, thus minimizing some of the fear and isolation. If a person isn't available as a resource, the little girl might choose a kind protective lion. When the abuser opened the door, perhaps to perpetrate additional abuse, the child could visualize the lion standing in front of her and scaring the attacker away. Any strengthening resource, person, or animal can assist the client in offsetting some of the intolerable emotions that may accompany the processing of the traumatic memory.

An additional technique attaches a positive, affirming statement to a pleasant visual image. For instance, Rita felt unloved by her earthly father, but she could effectively use her faith in Jesus as a resource. She visualized herself sitting in a beautiful flower garden with Jesus gazing lovingly at her with gentle compassionate eyes.

While visualizing this image she would affirm to herself, *"I am precious"* or *"I am loved."* Eye movements would seal this image and affirmation together. While using EMDR to overcome the negative memory and affect, she would bring this positive reinforcement into the process as needed. Resource Development and Installation can be as creative as required, but is definitely a valuable supplement to EMDR.

VISUAL IMAGERY

Visual images are either pleasant or unpleasant pictures in the mind that evoke various emotions associated with the scene that is being experienced. All images stimulate changes in the client's physiological state which are beneficial or detrimental. If a client is imagining herself resting by a babbling brook under the flowering branches of a pink dogwood tree, then that scene probably produces a calming effect on her physiological condition. If the image contains sights of a traumatic situation, then the bodily state is aroused and ready for action.

Clients can be taught to construct meaningful images that generate a relaxed state, even if it exists only for a short period of time. Trauma clients already know the power of images since their mind and memories are bombarded by intrusive content that they wish they didn't remember. Imagery can serve as a positive form of dissociation if the client can discover safe or relaxing places they can visit in their mental trips. Perhaps completely unfamiliar images would be helpful, so as not to stir up any reminders of the trauma. For instance, the client could project herself into a foreign country, or see herself on a mountain top (since she's not a hiker) or visualize herself in a refreshing botanical garden where there are few reminders of the familiar. Dissociating in this manner can provide a short reprieve, or mini-vacation, from the constancy of the trauma.

LOGOTHERAPY

Dr. Viktor Frankl (1959), a psychiatrist, originated logotherapy from his experiences as a prisoner in the Auschwitz concentration camp. He believes that a search for meaning is part of the essence of our human spirit and essential for survival. Trauma survivors seem to intuitively know that their prolonged and tedious pathway will take them on a search for meaning. Frankl explains that survivors of the Nazi concentration camps were stripped of everything except the last human freedom *"the ability to choose one's attitude in a given set of circumstances."* In comparing those who survived and those who died in the concentration camps, Frankl discovered that the survivors had managed to find a meaning to life even in those humiliating and devastating circumstances. Their attitude made the difference in the life or death quest. Frankl (1984) also explains that each person must find his or her own personal meaning, and meaning cannot be transferred from one person to another. At different points in life and at various ages, the meaning can vary. Any personal suffering sets humans on a quest for meaning.

Frankl uses the term *"tragic optimism,"* which he defines as the ability to transform suffering into a meaningful experience and to acquire a positive outlook on life's traumatic events. Not all clients will be able to achieve Frankl's honorable goals; however, considerable progress can be made if clients purpose in their hearts to create something notable from their pain. Numerous organizations were born from traumatic circumstances. Mothers Against Drunk Drivers (MADD) is one such organization. It was started by Candy Lightner whose young daughter was killed by a drunk driver. The Grief Recovery Institute is another. It was born out of the pain of personal losses from its two founders, John James and Russel Friedman. Heartbeat, a group of suicide survivors, was started by LaRita Archibald following the suicide of her twenty four year old son. Some trauma survivors may start a support group; others may write a book, poem, or music. The meaning and creativity that comes forth is as unique as the individual himself.

Dr. Frankl (1984) summed it up in the following statement: *"To weave these slender threads of a broken life into a firm pattern of meaning and responsibility is the object and challenge of logotherapy."* It has been said and it certainly applies to trauma survivors, *"Search for meaning, not happiness, and happiness may follow as a byproduct."*

VISUAL/KINESTHETIC DISSOCIATION (V/KD)

Although most dissociation is viewed as a detrimental side effect of trauma, there are some positive therapeutic forms of dissociation. V/KD has it's roots in Neurolinguistic Programming and employs a *"distancing"* effect both for visual and kinesthetic stimulants. It can be used effectively to process material that is so traumatic that the client might dissociate in an attempt to bear it. The distancing effect enables the client to process the visual and kinesthetic aspects of the trauma from a less provocative viewpoint.

The following basic steps can easily be applied.

1. Therapist instructs the client to pretend she is sitting in a movie theatre which features her life on the screen. Perhaps the client may choose to view the film in black and white to make it less real or threatening. The therapist will be upstairs in the projection room running the film.

2. The client will view some scenes that existed immediately before the trauma and led up to it.

3. When the film reaches the time and place of the trauma, the client will quickly vacate her seat and float up into the projection room with the therapist. The change in location provides *distance* and *support* for the client, thus dissociating the client from the event.

4. The client is asked to view the person that is down there on the screen (who, of course, is the self experiencing the trauma). The client is now observing as though the trauma was happening to someone else. If it was a childhood trauma, the therapist might say, *"see that little girl at the appropriate age. For instance, visualize three year old Alice riding her tricycle. She sees the dog, tries to run in the house, but gets bitten on her leg. See the frightened face of little Alice as the dog bites her."* The therapist leads the client all the way through the trauma.

5. The therapist may now request the client to rewind the movie as quickly as possible, within a few seconds. In other words, the client views the movie backwards. Alice screams and looks frightened, she is bitten by the dog, the dog is running backwards, Alice is running away from the house, etc..

6. The therapist asks the client if she has rewound it to the best of her ability. The rapidity of the procedure often enables the client to remove herself from the picture and obtain her freedom. Sometimes a piece of humor or bizarreness may even surface. If clients can dissociate from their feelings, they may not receive the emotional trigger from the amygdala, which is the usual PTSD response. The rapidity of this process may change or bypass the resultant feeling, which frees them from reliving the experience.

7. The therapist now asks if the client can sit in a seat close to the front of the theatre and view the movie. The client tries it and the therapist asks, *"Are there areas you didn't notice before?"* Discussion ensues. Sometimes a client may want to fast forward and run through it; or maybe they want to process one scene at a time. At any rate, the fast movement of this technique hopefully bypasses the feelings of the amygdala and frees the person from the accompanying PTSD emotional response.

TRAUMATIC INCIDENT REDUCTION (TIR)

French, G.D. & Harris, C.J. (1998) state that Traumatic Incident Reduction

> is a procedure intended to render benign the consequences of past traumatic events. Used correctly and in suitable circumstances, it eliminates virtually all of the symptoms of PTSD listed in the DSM-IV and is capable of resolving a host of painful and unwanted feelings and emotions that have not surrendered to other interventions.

TIR requires flexible therapeutic sessions in that the therapist or facilitator desires to have the client reach an end point, which results in better feelings. It is not unusual for a session to continue for two to three hours. The ideal situation would bring the client to a resolution with accompanying relief, brightening of facial features, and positive feelings in one session. The average session is about an hour and a half.

The basic steps are explained by French, G.D. & Harris, C.J. (1998) in their book Traumatic Incident Reduction (TIR). The following Basic TIR is the form used most frequently with traumatized clients. It consists of the following steps:

BASIC TIR*

1. *Consulting your client's interests, you select an incident to "run" or address.* Of course, in almost any case presenting with—and because of—a known, single-incident trauma such as a rape or a plane crash, this assessment is essentially done before you

---

* CRC Press LLC, 2000 Corporate Blvd. N.E., Boca Raton, FL 33431. Reprinted with permission from CRC Press LLC 1999, Traumatic Incident Reduction (TIR), Gerald D. French & Chrys J. Harris, Boca Raton, FL.

have begun, and the presenting incident is the one you will be running with your client.

2. *Find out where the incident happened.* You may get responses such as, "It was when we lived in Virginia," "It happened at Mom's house," "I was on the red eye flight from California," or "We were at Uncle Jack's farm." Any response indicating a place is acceptable.

3. *Find out how long the incident lasted.* Responses such as, "It lasted for fifteen minutes," "I was in it for over an hour," "We were only there for a few moments," or "It was just long enough for me to smoke a cigarette," would all be acceptable.

4. *Have your client focus on the moment the incident occurred.* You are asking your client to prepare for the TIR viewing by putting attention on the beginning of the incident.

5. *Have your client close his/her eyes (if it is comfortable to do so).* Closing eyes often helps the viewer "see" the incident more clearly by removing the distractions of the environment.

6. *Ask your client to describe the scene at the moment when the incident began.* This begins the description of the incident but it is only the beginning moment (to set the stage, so to speak).

7. *Have your client silently (re) "view" the incident from beginning to end.* Before your client begins to tell what happened, (s)he must put it into perspective. This silent viewing helps.

8. *Have the client tell you what happened.* Your client's answer to this instruction may be a spare outline, or it may be very detailed.

9. *Repeat steps 4, 7, and 8.*

From this point, you facilitate the viewing by having the client repeat the cycle of going to the start of the incident, moving through it silently to the end, and then telling you what happened (steps 4, 7, and 8) until the client reaches an end point.

Although the process seems simple, TIR does require special training and the Institute in Florida should be contacted as to dates and places of training.

EXPOSURE THERAPY

Exposure therapy is a form of desensitization where the client is systematically exposed to a feared memory, object, or anxiety provoking situation. One painful situation in life such as little Alice being bitten by a dog, may set up a conditioned anxiety response whenever she is exposed to a similar painful stimulus. Since Alice experienced a traumatizing canine attack with several bite marks from a friend's dog in the past, then even as an adult all dogs in the present may be approached as fearsome objects. If Alice had been attacked several times by the friend's dog, then the memory would be heightened and strengthened. Of course, the anxiety levels would greatly increase with each repeated assault. Alice would have acquired some automatic thoughts in the presence of this animal. *"See dog, get bit"* might become the dominating thought pattern. Even if she saw two harmless tiny puppies bouncing, tumbling, and rolling around with each other, the fear/anxiety response could surface. It is possible that this conditioned response would generalize itself to other animals as well, such as cats and kittens.

Even if the attacking dog was placed in a cage with secure locks, Alice would express discomfort in that dog's presence. Her intellect would tell her she is safe but the automatic thought would generate the conditioned response of fear and anxiety. Alice may live by the dictates of *"see dog, get bit."* She won't visit friends with dogs, jog in the nearby park where people walk their dogs, or garden in her front yard where neighbors' dogs would approach her.

Desensitization in the form of exposure therapy could assist Alice. The natural tendency would be to avoid all dogs, the therapeutic advice would be the opposite. She should gradually begin to approach dogs in a careful calculated manner. The therapist could begin by exposing her to pictures of dogs, perhaps fluffy innocent looking puppies. The next step might be viewing a short clip of a video with a child playing with a puppy. Perhaps brief exposure to a caged and tiny, friendly puppy with a wagging tail and wiggly body would then follow. Petting the back end of the puppy while the mouth is muzzled could increase the exposure at another session. Gradually Alice would increase the exposure by petting the puppy without a muzzle, and when comfortable could begin exposure work with larger dogs.

Imaginal exposure is another facet of this therapy. Revisiting a traumatic memory in a safe environment reduces the negative impact of the event. Harry, a Vietnam veteran, discovered that he had difficulty picnicking at a state park with his wife and children. Picnicking was a family outing that he had previously enjoyed and was surprised at his traumatic response to this seemingly innocuous outing. The family spread a blanket on the ground by a babbling brook just a short distance off the road. A rambunctious teenage boy raced by and his car backfired. This auditory stimulation set up a chain of events that were unexpected by Harry. The creek became a ditch where soldiers hid and exchanged gun fire with the enemy. The picnic blanket transformed itself into a covering for dead comrades. Harry relived the horror of the war experience and was visibly shaken. He sought counseling and repeatedly revisited the Vietnam experience with all the sights and sounds in a safe environment with the counselor. The imagined exposure gradually desensitized him.

GESTALT

Gestalt therapy originated by Fritz Perls (1969) is defined by Reber (1995) in the Penguin Dictionary of Psychology as treatment which

> focuses on attempts to broaden a person's awareness of self by using past experiences, memories, emotional states, bodily sensations, etc.. In short, everything that could contribute to the person forming a meaningful configuration of awareness is an acceptable part of the therapy process.

The *"empty chair"* or the *"invisible person in the chair"* technique has been highly popularized as a means of facilitating unexpressed or repressed emotion. For instance, Jerry could pretend that the chosen person (living or deceased) is seated in front of him and he would initiate a conversation, thus facilitating the needed expression. It can be a one-way conversation or Jerry can role play the other person.

In relationship to trauma or PTSD, a client may chose to put the *"numbness"* in an empty chair and give it a voice. The client may query the lack of feeling and ask what purpose it serves. The client may play the part of numbness and speak for it, thus providing awareness for the self. The startle response, hyperalertness, nightmares, or any symptoms could be challenged and explored with the empty chair technique.

It is also important to recognize that the self consists of roles we play. Roles demystify labels such as multiple personalities. It normalizes the split parts of the self. Fragmented parts of the self could be placed in the chair and their purpose and character investigated. From this awareness work, the client may view various personalities as expressions of the core self and not as separate entities. These parts can then be integrated into the core self.

Frequently, abused children or women lack assertiveness skills, and their survival was based on submission. That requirement squelched the self-protective mechanisms and emotions that normally would have surfaced. Role playing can strengthen their ability to stand up for themselves and to vent the anger and other accompanying emotions.

CHAPTER SIX

Compassion Fatigue

THE EFFECTS OF COMPASSION FATIGUE

Compassion Fatigue (CT), also known as Secondary Traumatic Stress, affects a broad range of health care professionals as well as others who provide a myriad of listening and support services. This condition occurs when professionals, families, friends, or care-givers are continually exposed to extreme emotional circumstances either directly or indirectly, in an attempt to treat or support trau-matized people.

Because the effects of compassion fatigue are cumulative, care-givers may be unaware of this syndrome's ability to rob them of their energy, vitality, and resiliency. The pervasiveness of this phe-nomenon places the helping professions at high risk of sacrificing their own physical, mental, emotional, and spiritual well-being on the *altars of compassion*.

COMPASSION FATIGUE AND BURNOUT

The logical question regarding the diagnosis of CT is whether or not it is the same condition as burnout. Maslach (1982) who developed the Maslach Burnout Inventory (MBI), provides an expla-nation for what he labeled as burnout. He indicates that this physi-cal, mental, and emotional exhaustion is caused by a depletion of the ability to cope with one's environment. This inability results from having to meet high level demands in daily life. Maslach's definition relates primarily to an environmental condition that considers numerous factors. The term Compassion Fatigue differs in that it concentrates on the transfer of emotions from the primary victim to a secondary one.

Figley (1995) provides a further comparison between burnout and Compassion Fatigue. Burnout

> emerges gradually . . . STS (secondary traumatic stress) can emerge suddenly with little warning . . . in contrast to burnout, there is a sense of helplessness and confusion, and a sense of isolation from supporters; the symptoms are often disconnected from real causes."

This concept of Compassion Fatigue is relatively new, entering our awareness with C. Joinson's (1992) article, "Coping with Compassion Fatigue" published by Nursing magazine. The article focused on describing the characteristics and behaviors of nurses who handled emergencies and developed compassion fatigue as a result.

Joinson is credited with the introduction of the term Compassion Fatigue, and others have contributed closely related concepts such as vicarious traumatization (McCann & Pearlman 1990) and secondary survivor (Remer & Elliott 1988b). Charles Figley (1995) popularized the term Compassion Fatigue when he used it as the title of his ground-breaking book. He also described this same phenomenon as Secondary Traumatic Stress (1983, 1985).

Figley (1995) defines Compassion Fatigue or Secondary Traumatic Stress as

> The natural behaviors and emotions that arise from know-ing about a traumatizing event experienced by a significant other—the stress resulting from helping or wanting to help a traumatized person.

EXAMPLES OF COMPASSION FATIGUE BURNOUT SYMPTOMS*

Cognitive

Lowered concentration, Decreased self-esteem, Apathy, Rigidity, Disorientation, Perfectionism, Minimization, Preoccupation with trauma, Thoughts of self-harm or harm to others.

Emotional

---

* Copyright 2002 Treating Compassion Fatigue, Charles R. Figley. Reproduced by permission of Routledge/Taylor & Francis Books, Inc..

Powerlessness, Anxiety, Guilt, Anger/rage, Survivor guilt, Shutdown, Numbness, Fear, Helplessness, Sadness, Depression, Emotional roller coaster, Depleted, Overly sensitive.

Behavioral

Inpatient, Irritable, Withdrawn, Moody, Regression, Sleep disturbance, Nightmares, Appetite changes, Hypervigilance, Elevated startle response, Accident proneness, Losing things.

Spiritual

Questioning the meaning of life, Loss of purpose, Lack of self-satisfaction, Pervasive hopelessness, Anger at God, Questioning of prior religious beliefs, Loss of faith in a higher power, Greater skepticism about religion.

Personal Relations

Withdrawal, Decreased interest in intimacy or sex, Mistrust, Isolation from others, Overprotection as a parent, Projection of anger or blame, Intolerance, Loneliness, Increased interpersonal conflicts.

Somatic

Shock, Sweating, Rapid heartbeat, Breathing difficulties, Aches and pains, Dizziness, Increased number and intensity of medical maladies, Other somatic complaints, Impaired immune system.

Work Performance

Low morale, Low motivation, Avoiding tasks, Obsession about details, Apathy, Negativity, Lack of appreciation, Detachment, Poor work commitments, Staff conflicts, Absenteeism, Exhaustion, Irritability, Withdrawal from colleagues.

Any of these symptoms could be signaling the presence of Compassion Fatigue Burnout.

AVOIDING COMPASSION FATIGUE

Figley believes that this syndrome could be classified as Secondary Traumatic Stress (STS) or in severe cases as Secondary Traumatic Stress Disorder (STSD). STS or STSD results from an intense and caring involvement with a traumatized person. In his 1995 book titled, Compassion Fatigue, he describes it as

> a state of tension and preoccupation with individual or cumulative trauma of clients as manifested in one or more ways: reexperiencing the traumatic events, avoidance/numbing or reminders of the event, (or) persistent arousal.

This description with the three clusters of reexperiencing, avoidance, and arousal sounds familiar in that they are Criterion B, Criterion C, and Criterion D of the DSM-IV-TR for PTSD.

The DSM-IV-TR (2000) cites two pathways from which PTSD can develop: direct or indirect exposure. Figley (1995) postulates that any individuals, (lay, volunteers, professional, or family) who are emotionally connected to the primary victim are vulnerable to develop Secondary Traumatic Stress Disorder. In relationship to health care professionals, it is highly likely that we can catch it from our clients. A good relationship between client and clinician depends on the clinician's ability to convey compassion, therefore rendering the clinician susceptible to secondary traumatic stress. Numerous theories have surfaced in an attempt to explain the mechanism by which this syndrome is transmitted, but there is no conclusive proof. Figley (1995) has hypothesized that indeed it is the empathy level of the clinician that causes the transmission and that assumption has certainly been validated in the lives of traumatized clinicians. An additional contributing factor lies in the background of many clinicians and caregivers. Approximately two-thirds of them are trauma survivors. That position renders them susceptible for retraumatization if preventive strategies are not employed.

Not only does a clinician personally suffer from the effects of Compassion Fatigue, but the professionalism of the clinician declines as well. For instance, Baranowsky (2002) and Danielli (1984) explain that clinicians find it difficult to listen to the traumatic experiences of the client and they redirect the conversation to material that is less anxiety provoking for themselves. The term for redirecting the conversation away from distressing information is called the Silencing Response. When used, it is indicative of the clinician's inability to handle the overwhelming nature of the client's story. Obviously, clinical efficiency is compromised at that point.

Self assessment is essential for all caregivers in the field of traumatology. Periodic checkups with another competent professional can also assist with some objectivity. The Compassion Satisfaction/Fatigue Self-Test for Helpers developed by B. Hudnall

Stamm and Charles R. Figley (1996) can be administered and self graded from time to time. Copies can be made of the test which allows the clinician to track the experience and compare scores, however, sale of the test is prohibited. Please see Appendix for a copy of the test.

All elements measured are significant and will provide information in three areas: compassion, job satisfaction, and fatigue. It is important to recognize and evaluate the impact of job satisfaction in addition to compassion and fatigue. Job satisfaction can serve as a powerful antidote against the effects of Compassion Fatigue.

It is important for clinicians to learn to recognize and combat the deleterious effects of STS, hopefully preventing the emergence of a subsequent disorder. Prevention, rather that treatment, must be addressed in a variety of ways. If we prevent Compassion Fatigue from occurring, there will be less need for treatment. Davis and Brody (1979) viewed prevention as primary, secondary, or tertiary. Primary deals with causes of social problems, secondary focuses on reducing violence or preparing for its effects, and tertiary concentrates on crisis intervention in the aftermath of violence. All of these components are important and clinicians are part of the greater community; however, some types of prevention are not under the direct control of the clinician. Self-responsibility and self care is mandatory for prevention of CT, while we all strive for prevention in the broader sense.

It is sometimes helpful for clinicians to pretend that they are giving advice to a client. What would we tell clients to do to offset stress in their lives? Frequently it is *"back to basics."* On a physical level, our recommendations would include such essentials as adequate sleep, proper nutrition, exercise, meditation, diaphragmatic breathing, relaxation, as well as numerous other health producing techniques mentioned in Chapter IV. Clinicians may also benefit from psychotherapeutic techniques such as EMDR, EFT, and Resource Installation. Other self soothers include journaling, poetry, art therapy, music therapy, recreation, time management, assertiveness, and stress inoculation training. A quick review of the therapeutic techniques in Chapters IV and V could benefit clinicians suffering from Compassion Fatigue.

In addition, many studies attest to the fact that humor can counteract the intensity of trauma work. Some work environments enjoy joke exchanges, where copies of jokes are placed in inboxes everyday to lighten the load. Fun should be liberally applied in offices, popcorn or treats could be served during serious meetings or discussions.

Breaks and lunches should be taken and restful places provided; mental health days should be offered. Institutions need to be worker friendly and sensitive to the needs of trauma care providers.

On a personal level, clinicians may need to take a trial-and-error approach in preventing and treating compassion fatigue. With the wealth of techniques and strategies available today, clinicians can pick, choose, and discard what doesn't work, and try again. Health care professionals of all occupations possess more knowledge on treating stress-related concerns than any other group or discipline. If we would practice what we preach, much compassion fatigue could be avoided.

If we frequently assess ourselves as thoroughly and accurately as we assess our clients, we will notice the early warning signals and ward off more serious implications. Ancient Biblical scriptures have encouraged us to *"Love thy neighbor as thyself."* Behaviorally, it appears that some health care professionals have interpreted the message differently. They live as though it said, *"Love thy neighbor instead of thyself."* If we don't appropriately love and respect ourselves, then we won't be able to love and give to trauma victims. Our compassion must be big enough and broad enough to encompass ourselves and others. Let's make a *"compassion"* commitment to ourselves to maintain our physical, mental, emotional, and spiritual health, so we can continue to offer life-giving compassion to others.

Appendix

COMPASSION SATISFACTION AND
FATIGUE (CSF) TEST*

Helping others puts you in direct contact with other people's lives. As you probably have experienced, your compassion for those you help has both positive and negative aspects. This self-test helps you estimate your compassion status: How much at risk you are of burnout and compassion fatigue and also the degree of satisfaction with your helping others. Consider each of the following characteristics about you and your current situation. Write in the number that honestly reflects how frequently you experienced these characteristics in the last week. Then follow the scoring directions at the end of the self-test.

0 = Never   1 = Rarely   2 = A few times

3 = Somewhat often   4 = Often   5 = Very often

Items About You

_____ 1. I am happy.

_____ 2. I find my life satisfying.

_____ 3. I have beliefs that sustain me.

_____ 4. I feel estranged from others.

_____ 5. I find that I learn new things from those I care for.

---

* Copyright 2002 from *Treating Compassion Fatigue* by Charles R. Figley. Reproduced by permission of Routledge/Taylor and Francis Books, Inc..

____ 6. I force myself to avoid certain thoughts or feelings that remind me of a frightening experience.

____ 7. I find myself avoiding certain activities or situations because they remind me of a frightening experience.

____ 8. I have gaps in my memory about frightening events.

____ 9. I feel connected to others.

____ 10. I feel calm.

____ 11. I believe I have a good balance between my work and my free time.

____ 12. I have difficulty falling or staying asleep.

____ 13. I have outbursts of anger or irritability with little provocation.

____ 14. I am the person I always wanted to be.

____ 15. I startle easily.

____ 16. While working with a victim, I thought about violence against the perpetrator.

____ 17. I am a sensitive person.

____ 18. I have flashbacks connected to those I help.

____ 19. I have good peer support when I need to work through a highly stressful experience.

____ 20. I have had first-hand experience with traumatic events in my adult life.

____ 21. I have had first-hand experience with traumatic events in my childhood.

____ 22. I think I need to "work through" a traumatic experience in my life.

____ 23. I think I need more close friends.

____ 24. I think there is no one to talk with about highly stressful experiences.

____ 25. I have concluded that I work too hard for my own good.

_____ 26. Working with those I help brings me a great deal of satisfaction.

_____ 27. I feel invigorated after working with those I help.

_____ 28. I am frightened of things a person I helped has said or done to me.

_____ 29. I experience troubling dreams similar to those I help.

_____ 30. I have happy thoughts about those I help and how I could help them.

_____ 31. I have experienced intrusive thoughts of times with especially difficult people I have helped.

_____ 32. I have suddenly and involuntarily recalled a frightening experience while working with a person I helped.

_____ 33. I am preoccupied with more than one person I help.

_____ 34. I am losing sleep over a person I help's traumatic experiences.

_____ 35. I have joyful feelings about how I can help the victims with whom I work.

_____ 36. I think that I might have been "infected" by the traumatic stress of those I help.

_____ 37. I think that I might be positively "inoculated" by the traumatic stress of those I help.

_____ 38. I remind myself to be less concerned about the well being of those I help.

_____ 39. I have felt trapped by my work as a helper.

_____ 40. I have a sense of hopelessness associated with working with those I help.

_____ 41. I have felt "on edge" about various things, and I attribute this to working with certain people I help.

_____ 42. I wish I could avoid working with some people I help.

_____ 43. Some people I help are particularly enjoyable to work with.

_____ 44. I have been in danger working with people I help.

_____ 45. I feel that some people I help dislike me personally.

Items About Being a Helper and Your Helping Environment

____ 46. I like my work as a helper.

____ 47. I feel I have the tools and resources that I need to do my work as a helper.

____ 48. I have felt weak, tired, and run down as a result of my work as helper.

____ 49. I have felt depressed as a result of my work as a helper.

____ 50. I have thoughts that I am a "success" as a helper.

____ 51. I am unsuccessful at separating helping from my personal life.

____ 52. I enjoy my coworkers.

____ 53. I depend on my coworkers to help me when I need it.

____ 54. My coworkers can depend on me for help when they need it.

____ 55. I trust my coworkers.

____ 56. I feel little compassion toward most of my coworkers.

____ 57. I am pleased with how I am able to keep up with helping technology.

____ 58. I feel I am working more for the money or prestige than for personal fulfillment.

____ 59. Although I have to do paperwork that I don't like, I still have time to work with those I help.

____ 60. I find it difficult separating my personal life from my helper life.

____ 61. I am pleased with how I am able to keep up with helping techniques and protocols.

____ 62. I have a sense of worthlessness/disillusionment/resentment associated with my role as a helper.

____ 63. I have thoughts that I am a "failure" as a helper.

____ 64. I have thoughts that I am not succeeding at achieving my life goals.

____ 65. I have to deal with bureaucratic, unimportant tasks in my work as a helper.

____ 66. I plan to be a helper for a long time.

Scoring Instructions

Please note that research is ongoing on this scale, and the following scores are theoretically derived and should be used only as a guide, not as confirmatory information.

1. Be certain you respond to all items.

2. Mark the items for scoring:

   a. Put an x by the following 26 items: 1–3, 5, 9–11, 14, 19, 26–27, 30, 35, 37, 43, 46–47, 50, 52–55, 57,59, 61, and 66.

   b. Put a check by the following 16 items: 17, 23–25, 41, 42, 45, 48, 49, 51, 56, 58, 60, and 62–65.

   c. Circle the following 23 items: 4, 6–8, 12, 13, 15, 16, 18, 20–22, 28, 29, 31–34, 36, 38–40, and 44.

3. Add the numbers you wrote next to the items for each set of items and note:

   a. *Your potential for compassion satisfaction (x):* 118 and above = extremely high potential; 100–117 = high potential; 82–99 = good potential; 64–81 = modest potential; below 63 = low potential.

   b. *Your risk for burnout (check):* 36 or less = extremely low risk; 37–50 = moderate risk; 51–75 = high risk; 76–85 = extremely high risk.

   c. *Your risk for compassion fatigue (circle):* 26 or less = extremely low risk; 27–30 = low risk; 31–35 = moderate risk; 36–40 = high risk; 41 or more = extremely high risk.

References

Adler, A. (1943). "Neuropsychiatric complications in victims of Boston's Coconut Grove disaster." *Journal of the American Medical Association*, 123, 1098–1101.

Allen, J.C. (1995). *Coping with Trauma, A Guide to Self-Understanding*, Washington, DC: American Psychiatric Press, Inc.

Armitage, R., Ruch, A.J., Trivedi, M., Cain, J., & Roffwarg, H.P. (1994). "The effects of nefazodone on sleep architecture in depression." *Neuropsychopharmacology* 10: 123–127.

Baranowsky, A.B. (2002). "The Silencing Response in Clinical Practice: On the Road to Dialogue." In *Treating Compassion Fatigue*, Charles R. Figley. New York: Brunner-Routledge.

Beck, A.T. (1976). *Cognitive Therapy and the Emotional Disorders*, New York: University Press.

Benson, H. (1975). *The Relaxation Response*, New York: Morrow Press.

Blank, A.S. (1993). *The longitudinal course of post-traumatic stress disorder. In J.R.T. Davidson, & E.B. Foa (Eds.) Post-traumatic stress disorder: DSM-IV and beyond,* (pp.3–22), Washington, DC.: American Psychiatric Press.

Brady, K., Pearlstein, T., Asnis G.M., Baker, D., Rothbaum, B., Sikes, C.R., & Farfel, G.M. (2000). "Efficacy and safety of sertraline treatment of posttraumatic stress disorder: A randomized controlled trial." *Journal of the American Medical Association*, 283, 1837–1844.

Brady, K.T., Sonne, S.C., & Roberts, J.M. (1995). "Sertraline treatment of comorbid posttraumatic stress disorder and alcohol dependence." *Journal of Clinical Psychiatry*, 56, 502–505.

Brady, K., Pearlstein, T., Asnis, G.M., Baker, D., Rothbaum, B., Sikes, C.R., & Farfel, G.M. (2000). "Efficacy and safety of sertraline treatment of posttraumatic stress disorder. A randomized controlled trial." *Journal of the American Medical Association*, 283, 1837–1844.

Brewin, C.R., Andrews, B., Rose, S., & Kirk, M. (1999). "Acute stress disorder and posttraumatic stress disorder in victims of violent crime." *American Journal of Psychiatry*, 156, 360–366.

Briere, J. (1997). *Psychological Assessment of Adult Posttraumatic States*, Washington, DC: American Psychological Association.

Bonhoeffer, M. (1926). "Beurteilung, Begutachtung, und Rechtsprechung bei den sogenanaten Unfollsneuroson." *Deutsche Medizinische Wochenschrife* ,52, 179–182.

Bremner, J.D. (2002). *Does Stress Damage the Brain?* New York: W. W. Norton & Co..

Bremner, J.D., Randall, P., Scott, T.M., Bronen, R.A., Seibyl, J.P., Southwick, W.M., Delaney, R.C., McCarthy, G., Charney, D.S., & Innis, R.B. (1995). "MRI-based measurement of hippocampus volume in post-traumatic stress disorder." *American Journal of Psychiatry*, 152, 973–981.

Bremner, J.D., Vermetten, E., & Mazure, C.M. (2000). "Development and preliminary psychometric properties of an instrument for the measurement of childhood trauma: The Early Trauma Inventory." *Depression and Anxiety*, 12, 1–12.

Bremner, J.D., Randall, P., Scott, T.M., Bronen, R.A., Seibyl, J.P., Southwick, S.M., Delaney, R.C., McCarthy, G., Charney, D.S., & Innis, R.B. (1995). "MRI-based measurement of hippocampal volume in posttraumatic stress disorder." *American Journal of Psychiatry*, 152, 973–981.

Bremner, J.D., Randall, P.R., Capelli, S., Scott, T., McCarthy, G., & Charney, D.S. (1995). "Deficits in short-term memory in adult survivors of childhood abuse." *Psychiatry Research*, 59, 97–107.

Bremner, J.D., Randall, P., Vermetten, E., Staib, L., Bronen, R.A., Capelli, S., Mazure, C.M., McCarthy, G., Innis, R.B., & Charney, D.S. (1997). "MRI-based measurement of hippocampal volume in posttraumatic stress disorder related to childhood physical and sexual abuse: A preliminary report." *Biological Psychiatry*, 41, 23–32.

Bremner, J.D., Narayan, M., Anderson, E.R., Staib, L.H., Miller, H., & Charney, D.S. (2000). "Hippocampal volume reduction in major depression." *American Journal of Psychiatry*, 157, 115–117.

Brickner, Sheryl (1999). "Emotional Freedom Techniques." *CoACCT Newsletter*.

Cannon, W.B. (1914). "The emergency function of the adrenal medulla in pain and the major stress emotions." *American Journal of Physiology*, 3, 356–372.

Cannon, W.B. (1927). "The James-Lange theory of emotions: A critical reappraisal and alternative theory." *Journal of Psychology*, 39, 106–124.

Craig, G., & Fowlie, A. (1995). *Emotional Freedom Techniques: The Manual*. The Sea Ranch, CA.

Danielli, Y. (1984). "Psychotherapists participation in the conspiracy of silence about the Holocaust." *Psychoanalytic Psychology*, 1 (1), 23–42.

Davidson, J.H., Kudler, H., Smith, R. et al. (1990). "Treatment of post-traumatic stress disorder with amitryptyline and placebo." *Arch. Gen. Psychiatry* 47: 259–266.

Davidson, J.R.T., Malik, M.L., & Sutherland, S.M. (1996). "Response characteristics to antidepressants and placebo in post-traumatic stress disorder." *International Clinical Psychopharmacology*, 12, 291–296.

Davidson, J. & Van der Kolk, B. (1996). The psychopharmacological treatment of posttraumatic stress disorder. In B.A. Van der Kolk, A.C. McFarlane, & L. Weisaeth (Eds.) *Traumatic stress: The effects of overwhelming experience on mind, body, and society* (pp. 510–524). New York: Guilford Press.

Davis, M. (1992). "The role of the amygdala in fear and anxiety." *Annual Reviews of Neuroscience*, 15, 353–375.

Davis, L.J. & Brody, E.W. (1979). Rape and older women: A guide to preventional protection. U.S. Department of Health and Welfare, National Institute of Mental Health, DHHS Publication No. ADM 78–734.

DeBoer, M.C., Opden Velde, W., Falger, P.R.J., Hovens, J.E., DeGroen, J.H.M., & Van Duijn, H. (1992). "Fluvoxamine treatment for chronic PTSD: A pilot study." *Psychotherapy and Psychosomatics*, 57, 158–163.

Diagnostic and Statistical Manual of Mental Disorders, Fourth Edition, Text Revision. (2000). Washington, DC: American Psychiatric Association.

Ellis, A. (1962). *Reason and Emotion in Psychotherapy*, New York: Stuart Press.

Figley, C.R., & Carbonell, J. (1995). "The 'Active Ingredient' Project: the systematic clinical demonstration of the most efficient treatments of PTSD, a research plan." Tallahassee: Florida State University Psychosocial Stress Research Program and Clinical Laboratory, in Gallo, *Energy Psychology*. Washington, DC: CRC Press.

Figley, C.R. (1995). *Compassion Fatigue: Coping with Secondary Traumatic Stress Disorder in Those Who Treat the Traumatized*. New York: Brunner/Mazel.

Figley, C.R., & Stamm, B.H. (1996). "Psychometric Review of the Compassion Fatigue Self Test." In B.H. Stamm (Ed.), *Measurement of Stress, Trauma and Adaptation*, Lutherville, MD: Sidran Press.

Figley, C.R.(2002). *Treating Compassion Fatigue*. New York: Brunner/Mazel

Foa, E.B., Davidson, J.R.T., & Frances, A. (Eds.). 1999). "The expert consensus guideline series: Treatment of posttraumatic stress disorder." *Journal of Clinical Psychiatry*, 60 (Suppl. 16), 1–18.

Frankl, V. (1959). *From death camp to existent lives*. New York: Beacon Press.

Frankl, V. (1984). *Man's Search for Meaning* (3rd Ed.). New York: Pocket Books.

French, G.D., & Harris, C.J. (1998). *Traumatic Incident Reduction*, Boca Raton, FL: CRC Press LLC.

Freud, S. (1955). *Beyond the pleasure principle* (pp.29–33). Standard Edition, Vol. 18, (original work published 1920), London: Hogarth Press.

Friedman, M.J. & Southwick, S.M. (1995). "Towards pharmacotherapy for PTSD." M.J. Friedman, D.S. Charney & A.Y. Deutch (Eds.), *Neurobiologic and Clinical Consequences of Stress: From Normal Adapation to PTSD* (pp. 465–481). Philadelphia, PA: Lippincott-Raven Press.

Friedman, M.J. (1990). Interrelationships between biological mechanisms and pharmacotherapy of posttraumatic stress disorder. In M.E. Wolfe & A.D. Mosnaim (Eds.), *Post-Traumatic Stress Disorder: Etiology, Phenomenology, and Treatment* (pp. 204–225). Washington, DC: American Psychiatric Press.

Friedman, M.J. (2001). *Post-Traumatic Stress Disorder: The Latest Assessment and Treatment Strategies*. Kansas City, MO: Dean Psych. Press Corp. a/b/a Compact Clinicals.

Gentry, Eric J. (2002). *Instructional Manual* (Version 4.3). Tampa FL: Traumatology Institute.

Gould, E., Tanapat, P., McEwen, B.S., Flugge, G., & Fuchs, E. (1998). "Proliferation of granule cell precursors in the dentate gyrus of adult monkeys is diminished by stress." *Proceedings of the National Academy of Sciences USA*, 95, 3168–3171.

Guralnik, D.B. (1970). *Webster's New World Dictionary of the American Language*, Nashville, TN: The World Publishing Co.

Hearst, P.C. & Moscow, A. (1982). *Every Secret Thing*, New York: Doubleday.

Herman, J.L. (1992). *Trauma and Recovery*. New York: Basic Books.

Hilberman, E. (1980). "The 'wife-beater's wife' reconsidered." *Am. J. Psychiatry*, 137, 1336–1347.

Hobson, J.A. (1994). *The Chemistry of Conscious States: How the Brain Changes its Mind*. New York: Little, Brown.

Horowitz, M. (1999) *Introduction—Essential Papers on Posttraumatic Stress disorder*, New York, NY: University Press.

Horowitz, M. (1986). *Stress Response Syndromes*. New York, NY: Jason Aronsom.

Hudgins, K.M. (2002). *Experiential Treatments for PTSD, The Therapeutic Spiral Model*. New York, NY: Springer Publishing Co., Inc..

Inman, D.J., Silver, S.M. & Doghramji, K. (1990). "Sleep disturbance in post-traumatic stress disorder: A comparison with non-PTSD insomnia." *J. Traumatic Stress* 3: 429–437.

Jacobs, S. C. (1999). *Traumatic Grief: Diagnosis, Treatment, and Prevention*. Castleton, NY: Hamilton Printing Co.

Joinson, C. (1992). "Coping with compassion fatigue." *Nursing*, 22 (4), 116–122.

Kernberg, O. (1967). "Borderline personality organization." *J. Am. Psychoanal. Assoc.*, 15, 641–685.

Kessler, R.C., Sonnega, A., Bromet, E., Hughes, M., & Nelson, C.B. (1995). "Posttraumatic stress disorder in the national comorbidity survey." *Archives of General Psychiatry*, 52, 1048–1060.

Kinzie, J.D. & Leung, P. (1989). "Clonidine in Cambodian patients with posttraumatic stress disorder." *Journal of Nervous and Mental Disease*, 177, 546–550.

Kolb, L.C., Burris, B.C., & Griffiths, S. (1984). "Propranolol and clonidine in the treatment of the chronic post-traumatic stress disorders of war." In B.A. van der Kolk (Ed.), *Post-traumatic Stress Disorder: Psychological and biological sequelae* (pp. 97–107). Washington, DC: American Psychiatric Press.

Kramer, M.S., Schoen, L.S., & Kinney, L. (1984). "The dream experience in dream disturbed Vietnam veterans." In *Post-traumatic Stress Disorders: Psychological and Biological Sequelae*. B. van der Kolk, Ed. Washington, DC: American Psychiatric Press.

Krystal, H. (Ed.) (1968). *Massive psychic trauma*. New York: International Universities Press.

Lazarus, R. (1984). "Puzzles in the Study of Daily Hassles." *Journal of Behavioral Medicine*. 7: 375–389.

Le Chapman, W.P., Schroeder, H.R., Guyer, G., Brazier, M.A.B., Fager, C., Poppen, J.L., Solomon, H.C., & Yakolev, P.I. (1954) "Physiological evidence concerning the importance of the amygdaloid nuclear region in the integration of circulating functions and emotion in man." *Science*, 729, 949–950.

LeDoux, J.E. (1993). Emotional memory systems in the brain. *Behavioral and Brain Research*, 58, 69–79.

Leeds, A.M. (1999). "Principles of case formulation and use of EMDR Resource Development and installation in the treatment of complex posttraumatic stress disorder and adults with insecure attachment status." EMDR Institute: Level 2 Specialty Presentation, Denver, CO.

Lerner, Mark D. (2002). *An Overview of Experts in Traumatic Stress, Trauma Response*. New York: The American Academy of Experts in Traumatic Stress, Inc., www.aaets.org.

Lindy, J.D. (1985). "The trauma membrane and other concepts derived from psychotherapeutic work with survivors of natural disaster." *Psychiatric Annals*, 15 (3), 153–160.

Lifton, R.J., & Olson, E. (1976). "The Human Meaning of Total Disaster, The Buffalo Creek Experience." *Psychiatry*, 39, 1–18. Guilford Press. In *Essential Papers on Posttraumatic Stress Disorder,* Horowitz, Mardi, M.D. (1999). New York, NY: New York University Press.

Lindemann, E. (1944). "Symptomatology and management of acute grief." *American Journal Psychiatry*, 101: 141–148.

Lindy, J.D. (1996). "Psychoanalytic psychotherapy of post-traumatic stress disorder: The nature of the therapeutic relationship." In B. van der Kolk, A. McFarlane, & L. Weisaeth (Eds.) *Traumatic stress: The Effects of Overwhelming Experience on Mind, Body, and Society* (pp. 525–536), New York; Guilford Press.

Lindy, J.D., & Wilson, J.P. (2001). "Respecting the trauma membrane: Above all, do no harm." In *Treating Psychological Trauma & PTSD*. New York: Guilford Press.

Lovelace, L., & McGrady, M. (1980). *Ordeal*, Secaucus, NJ: Citadel.

Maslach, C. (1982). *The Burnout: The Cost of Caring*. Englewood Cliffs, N.J.: Prentice-Hall.

McCann, I.L., & Pearlman, L.A. (1990). "Vicarious traumatization: A framework for understanding the psychological effects of working with victims." *Journal of Traumatic Stress*, 3 (1), 131–150.

McEwen, B.S., Angulo, J., Cameron, H., Chao, H.M., Daniels, D., Gannon, M.N., Gould, E., Mendelson, S., Sakai, R., Spencer, R., & Wooley, C. (1992). "Paradoxical effects of adrenal steroids on the brain: Protection versus degeneration." *Biological Psychiatry*, 31, 177–199.

McEwen, B.S., Conrad, C.D., Kuroda, Y., Frankfurt, M., Magarinos, A.M., & McKittrick, C. (1997). "Prevention of stress-induced morphological and cognitive consequences." *European Neuropsychopharmacology*, 7 (3), 322–328.

McFarlane, A.C., Weber, D.L., & Clark, C.R. (1993). "Abnormal stimulus processing in post-traumatic stress disorder." *Biological Psychiatry*, 34, 311–320.

Mellman, T.A., Kulick-Bell, R., Ashlock, L.E. & Nolan, B (1995). "Sleep events in combat-related post traumatic stress disorder." *Am. J. Psychiatry* 152: 110–115.

Niederland, W.G. (1968). "Clinical observations on the 'survivor syndrome.'" *Int. J. Psychoanal.*, 49, 313–315.

Ogden, P., Minton, K. (2000) "Sensorimotor psychotherapy: One method for processing trauma." *Traumatology*, 6(3), article 3 (October 2000) at www.fse.edu/-trauma/v6i3a3.html.

Pennebaker, J.W., & Campbell, R.S. (2000). "The effects of writing about traumatic experience." *Clinical Quarterly* 9(2): 17, 19–21.

Perls, F.S. (1969). *Gestalt Therapy Verbatim*, Moab, UT: Real People Press.

Perry, B.D. (1994). "Neurobiological Sequelae of Childhood trauma: Post Traumatic stress disorders in children." In M. Murburg (Ed.), *Catecholamines in Posttraumatic Stress Disorder: Emerging Concepts* (pp. 233–276). Washington, DC: American Psychiatric Press.

Pert, C. (1997). *Mole of Emotions: Why You Feel the Way You Feel*, New York: Scribner.

Prigerson, H.G., Shear, M.K., Jacobs, S.C., Reynolds, C.F. III, Maciejewski, J.R., Davidson, J.R.T., Rosenheck, R., Pilkonis, P.A., Wortman, C.B., Williams, J.B.W., Widiger, T.A., Frank, E., Kupfer, D.J., & Zisook, S. (1999). "Consensus criteria for traumatic grief: A preliminary empirical test." *British Journal of Psychiatry*, 194, 67–73.

Prigerson, H.G., Maciejewski, P.K., Newsom, J., Reynolds, C.F., Frank, E., Bierhals, A.J., Miller, M.D., Fasiczka, A., Doman, J., & Houck, P.R. (1995b). "The inventory of complicated grief: A scale to measure maladaptive symptoms of loss." *Psychiatry Research*, 59, 65–79.

Prigerson, H. G., Vanderwerker, L. C., Maciejewski, P. K. (2007). "Prolonged Grief Disorder. Inclusion in DSM Complicated Grief as a Mental Disorder: Inclusion in DSM."(chapter 8). *Handbook of Bereavement Research and Practice: 21st Century Perspectives*, Eds., Margaret Stroebe, Robert Hansson, Henk Schut & Wolfgang Strobe, Washington, D.C.: American Psychological Association Press.

Putnam, F.W., et al. (1986). "The clinical phenomenology of multiple personality disorder: A review of 100 recent cases." *Journal of Clinical psychiatry*, 47, 283–293.

Rando, T.A. (1993). *Treatment of Complicated Mourning*, Champaign, IL: Research Press.

Raphael, B., & Wilson, J.P. (2000). "Psycho Therapeutic and Pharmacology Intervention for Bereaved Persons" (chapter 26). *Handbook of Bereavement Research, Diagnostic and Statistical Manual of Mental Disorders* (2000). Fourth Edition, Rev. Washington, DC: American Psychiatric Association.

Reber, A.S. (1995). *The Penguin Dictionary of Psychology* (2nd Ed.) London, England: Penguin Group.

Remer, R., & Elliot, J. (1988b). "Management of secondary victims of sexual assault." *International Journal of Family Psychiatry*, 9 (4), 389–400.

Resick, P.A. (2001). *Stress and Trauma*. Philadelphia, PA: Psychology Press.

Reynolds, C.F., Buysse, D.J., Kupper, D.J., Hoch, C.C., Houch, P.R., Matzzie, J., & George, C.J. (1990). "Rapid eye movement sleep deprivation as probe in elderly subjects." *Arch. Gen. Psychiatry* 47: 1128–1136.

Rieker, P.P. & Carmen, E. (1986). "The victim-to-patient process: The disconfirmation and transformation of abuse." *Am. J. Orthopsychiat.* 56, 360–370.

Ross, R.J., Ball, W.A., Dinges, D.F., Kribbs, N.B., Morrison, A.R., Silver, S.M., & Mulvaney, F.D. (1994). "Rapid eye movement sleep disturbance in posttraumatic stress disorder." *Biol. Psychiatry* 35: 195–202.

Sapolsky, R.M. (1996). "Why stress is bad for your brain." *Science*, 273,749–750.

Schupp, Linda J. (2003). *Grief: Normal, Complicated, and Traumatic*. Eau Claire, WI: PESI Healthcare.

Schupp, Linda J. (1992). *Is There Life After Loss?* Lakewood, CO.

Seaward, B.L. (1999). *Managing Stress: Principles and Strategies for Health and Well Being*. (2nd Ed.) Boston: Jones and Bartlett Publishers.

Selye, H. (1976). *The Stress of Life*. New York: McGraw-Hill. (Originally published in 1956.)

Shalev, Arieh Y. (1996). *"Stress versus Traumatic Stress: From Acute Homeostatic Reactions to Chronic Psychopathology"* In Van der Kolk, Bessel, McFarlane, Alexander C., and Weisaeth, Lars (eds.) *Traumatic Stress: The Effects of Overwhelming Experience on Mind, Body, and Society*, (pp. 83–85), New York: Guilford Press.

Shapiro, F. (1998). *EMDR level I training manual*. Pacific Grove, CA: EMDR Institute.

Shapiro, F. (1989). "Eye movement desensitization: A new treatment for post traumatic stress disorder." *Journal of Behavior Therapy and Experimental Psychiatry*, 20, 211–217.

Shapiro, F. (1995). *Eye movement desensitization and reprocessing: Basic principles, protocols, and procedures*. New York: Guilford.

Sheline, Y., Wang, P., Gado, M., Csernansky, J., & Vannier, M. (1996). "Hippocampal atrophy in major depression." *Proceedings of the National Academy of Sciences: USA*, 93, 3908–3913.

Siegel, B. (1986). *Love, Medicine, & Miracles*, New York: Harper & Row.

Sime, W.E, *Psychological benefits of exercise training in the healthy individual, in Behavioral Health: A Handbook of Health Enhancement and Disease Prevention*. Edited by Matarazzo, J.D., Weiss, S.M, Herd, J.A., et al. New York, Wiley, 1984, pp 488–508.

Smith, M.A., Makino, S., Kvetnansky, R., & Post, R.M. (1995). "Stress and glucocorticoids affect the expression of brain-derived neurotrophic factor and neurotrophin-e mRNA in the hippocampus." *Journal of Neuroscience,* 15, 1768–1777.

Stein, M.B., Koverola, C., Hanna, C., Torchia, M.G., & McClarty, B. (1997). "Hippocampal volume in women victimized by childhood sexual abuse." *Psychological Medicine,* 27, 951–959.

Stierlin, E. (1911). "Nervose und psychische stoning nach Katastrophen" (Nervous and psychic disturbances after catastrophes) *Deutsches Medizinische Worhenschrift,* 37, 2028–2035.

Southwick, S.M., Yehuda, R., Giller, El, et al. (1994). "Use of tricyclics and monoamine oxidase inhibitors in the treatment of PTSD: A quantitative review." M.M. Murburg (Ed.), *Catecholamine function in post-traumatic stress disorder: Emerging concepts* (pp. 293–305). Washington, DC: American Psychiatry Press.

Terr, L. (1994). *Unchained Memories: True Stories of Traumatic Memories Lost and Found,* New York: Basic Books.

Thompson, R. & Smith, C. (1993). "Trauma Touch Therapy," *Massage,* May/June, Davis, CA: Noah Publishing.

Timerman, J. (1981). *Prisoner Without a Name, Cell Without a Number,* (Trans. Talbot, T.), New York: Vintage.

Uno, H., Tarara, R., Else, J.G., Suleman, M.A., & Sapolsky, R.M. (1989). "Hippocampal damage associated with prolonged and fatal stress in primates." *Journal of Neuroscience,* 9, 1705–1711.

Van der Kolk, B.A., & Ducey (1989). "The psychological processing of traumatic experience: Rorschach patterns in PTSD." *Journal of Traumatic Stress,* 2(3) 259–274.

Van der Kolk, B.A., Burbridge, J.A., & Suzuki, J. (1997). "The psychobiology of traumatic memory." *Annals New York Academy of Science,* 99–110.

Van der Kolk, B.A., McFarlane, A.C., Weisaeth, W. (1996). *Traumatic Stress,* New York, NY: The Guilford Press.

Van der Kolk, B.A. (1987). *Psychological Trauma.* Washington, DC: American Psychiatric Press.

Van der Kolk, B.A. & Fisler, R. (1995). "Dissociation and the fragmentary nature of traumatic memories. Overview and exploratory study." *Journal of Traumatic Stress*, 9, 505–525.

Van der Kolk, B.A., Dryfuss, D., Michaels, M., Berkowitz, R., Saxe, G., & Goldenberg, I. (1994). "Fluoxetine in post-traumatic stress disorder." *Journal of Clinical Psychiatry*, 55, 517–522.

Westerlund, E. (1992). *Women's Sexuality After Childhood Incest,* New York: W. W. Norton.

Wilbarger, P. & Wilbarger, J. (1997). *Sensory defensiveness and related social/emotional and neurological problems*. Van Nuys, CA: Wilbarger.

Williams, M.B. & Poijula, S. (2002). *The PTSD Workbook: Simple, Effective Techniques for Overcoming Traumatic Stress,* Oakland, CA: New Harbinger Publications, Inc..

Yehuda, R., & McFarlane, A.C. (1995). "Conflict between current knowledge about posttraumatic stress disorder and its original conceptual basis." *American Journal of Psychiatry*, 152 (12), 1705–1713. American Psychiatric Association.

STUDY PACKAGE
CONTINUING EDUCATION
CREDIT INFORMATION

ASSESSING AND TREATING
TRAUMA AND PTSD

Thank you for choosing PESI, LLC as your continuing education provider. Our goal is to provide you with current, accurate and practical information from the most experienced and knowledgeable speakers and authors.

Listed below are the continuing education credit(s) currently available for this self-study package. ***Please note, your state licensing board dictates whether self study is an acceptable form of continuing education. Please refer to your state rules and regulations.*

Counselors: PESI, LLC is recognized by the National Board for Certified Counselors to offer continuing education for National Certified Counselors. Provider #: 5896. We adhere to NBCC Continuing Education Guidelines. This self-study package qualifies for 3.0 contact hours.

Psychologists: PESI, LLC is approved by the American Psychological Association to sponsor continuing education for psychologists. PESI, LLC maintains responsibility for this program and its content. PESI is offering this activity for 3 hours of continuing education credit.

Social Workers: PESI, LLC, 1030, is approved as a provider for social work continuing education by the Association of Social Work Boards (ASWB), (1-800-225-6880) through the Approved Continuing Education (ACE) program. PESI maintains responsibility for the program. Licensed Social Workers should contact their individual state boards to review continuing education requirements for licensure renewal. Social Workers will receive 3.0 continuing education clock hours for completing this self-study package.

Addiction Counselors: PESI, LLC is a Provider approved by NAADAC Approved Education Provider Program. Provider #: 366. This self-study package qualifies for 3.5 contact hours.

Procedures: 1. Read book.
                2. Complete the post-test/evaluation form and mail it along with payment to the address on the form.

Your completed test/evaluation will be graded. If you receive a passing score (80% and above), you will be mailed a certificate of successful completion with earned continuing education credits. If you do not pass the post-test, you will be sent a letter indicating areas of deficiency, references to the appropriate sections of the manual for review and your post-test. The post-test must be resubmitted and receive a passing grade before credit can be awarded.

If you have any questions, please feel free to contact our customer service department at 1-800-843-7763.

PESI, LLC
200 SPRING ST. STE B, P.O. BOX 100
EAU CLAIRE, WI 54702-1000

Product Number: ZHS008685   **CE Release Date:** 12/08/03

Assessing and Treating
Trauma and PTSD

P.O. Box 1000
Eau Claire, WI 54702
(800) 843-7763

ZNT008685

This home study package includes CONTINUING
EDUCATION FOR ONE PERSON: complete & return
this original post/test evaluation form.

ADDITIONAL PERSONS interested in receiving credit
may photocopy this form, complete and return with a
payment of $15.00 per person CE fee. A certificate of
successful completion will be mailed to you.

For office use only
Rcvd. _____
Graded _____
Cert. mld. _____

C.E. Fee: $15 Credit card # _____

Exp. Date _____

Signature _____

V-Code* _____ (***MC/VISA/Discover:** last 3-digit # on signature
panel on back of card.) (***American Express:** 4-digit # above account # on face
of card.)

**Mail to: PESI HealthCare, PO Box 1000, Eau Claire, WI 54702, or
Fax to: PESI HealthCare (800) 675-5026 (fax all pages)**

Name (please print): _____ _____ _____
　　　　　　　　　　　　　　　　　LAST　　　　　　　　　　　FIRST　　　　　　M.I.

Address: _____

City: _____ State: _____ Zip: _____

Daytime Phone: _____

Signature: _____

• Date you completed the PESI HC Tape/Manual Independent Package: _____

• Actual time (# of hours) taken to complete this offering: _____ hours

PROGRAM OBJECTIVES

How well did we do in communicating the following objectives?

	Excellent				Poor
Describe the etiology and impact of traumatic stress.	5	4	3	2	1
Assess the varied trauma-related disorders, conditions and treatment issues.	5	4	3	2	1
Develop a safe therapeutic environment by using comm-unication/counseling skills.	5	4	3	2	1
Utilize a variety of physiological interventions.	5	4	3	2	1
Apply previous and modern psychological treatments for traumatic stress.	5	4	3	2	1

POST-TEST QUESTIONS (TRUE OR FALSE)

1. Selective serotonin reuptake inhibitors (SSRIs) are considered by experts as the best psychopharmacological treatment for PTSD.

   True or **False**

2. The proposed criteria for Prolonged Grief Disorder may become a new diagnostic entity in the next Diagnostic and Statistical Manual of Mental Disorders.

   True or **False**

3. EMDR has more scientific research as a trauma treatment than any other method, except for medication.

   True or **False**

4. Atrophy of the hippocampus can cause problems with memory, new learning, and dissociation.

   True or **False**

5. Men develop PTSD after a traumatic event twice as often as women.

   True or **False**

For additional forms and information on other PESI products, contact:
**Customer Service; PESI HEALTHCARE; P.O. Box 1000; Eau Claire, WI 54702
(Toll Free, 7 a.m.-5 p.m. central time, 800-843-7763).
www.pesihealthcare.com**

Thank you for your comments.
We strive for excellence and we value your opinion.